INVERTED LEADERSHIP:

Lead Others Better By Forgetting About Yourself

Joel W. Hawbaker

Foreword by Dondi Scumaci

Dedication

This book is dedicated to my entire family and especially to my wife and children: Maryellyn, God has used you to restore my whole world even though I'm undeserving, and I'll always be grateful. Carly and Lou, words can't express what how grateful I am to have you two as my daughters. I love you all.

TABLE OF CONTENTS

Acknowledgements

This book would never have been possible without the help and encouragement of many people. If I happen to forget someone, I ask you to please forgive my oversight!

First, I'm thankful to our God, who is a God of grace and mercy as well as love and justice. I know better now just how much I could never repay or be worthy of what I've been given. Thank you for Jesus.

I'm also extremely grateful to my wife, who spent hours helping me type and revise the book, and who also spent even more hours listening to me complain about how much work it was. Before you, Mel, I'd never written anything. Thanks to you I've now written multiple articles, dozens of blog posts, an e-book about my dad, and this, my first full-length book. You're my muse, and I couldn't imagine doing this without you. Thank you more than I can say.

I also need to be sure to thank you to my daughters, both for enduring the conversations about the book and, more importantly, for being the reason I want to be a better leader. I'm already a better person because of you both, and I hope to become better still.

I'm grateful to my friends and family who helped me and who are present in the pages, whether they are named in the body of the book or not: David, Erik (thanks too for your cover quote!), John and Genia, Julie, Brian, Mom, Ted and Karen, Rick and Kinsey. I'm also grateful to my school administration for putting up with me working on my book sometimes during my planning period and for being so encouraging about the whole project: to Westbrook Christian School and the Big Oak Ranch Coach Kennedy, and Mrs. Greer.

Thanks also to my church family at Hope Community PCA in Jacksonville, Alabama, and especially to Pastor Steve Mayes for your faithful preaching of God's word every Sunday.

Thanks also to all of my students and soccer players over the years for being such a huge part of my life; and thank you to all of your parents for allowing me to be a part of yours.

Thank you to the many people who read the book and provided feedback on it (especially Beverly Haynes, Jamie Barrett, and Rene Zeringue); the book is most certainly better and the message more clearly expressed because of you.

I'm thankful to Dondi Scumaci, whose quote appears on the back cover, and to Bob Burg, whose influence is also felt throughout the pages here. Thanks to other thought leaders whose works have influenced me: Grant Baldwin (who first made influenced me to think about being a speaker and author), Jon Acuff, and Neen James. Thanks to Chandler Bolt (Self Publishing School) and Rob Kosburg (Best Seller Publishing) for all your help and great content in learning about writing and self-publishing a book.

Thanks to everyone who has been kind enough to help me publicize and promote the book! Your efforts have helped me reach far more people than I'd have reached on my own, and I'm extremely grateful.

Finally, thank you, the reader, for taking the time to read my book. I'm honored and humbled, and I hope you find it was worth the effort to read it.

Foreword

When I read *Inverted Leadership*, my first thought was how absolutely refreshing this message is. (I think the world needs more stories like this one. Yes, please!) Beyond refreshing, this book is encouraging, inspiring and actionable. As I read, I found myself asking, "Who is this written for?" The further I read, the longer the list became. *Inverted Leadership* is for every:

- Child who didn't have a father's example
- Person who has lost a parent (and continues to find ice scrapers in the toolbox: you'll read more about this later!), reminding them of the endless ways they were cared for and loved
- Parent aspiring to equip children with the disciplines to build a meaningful life
- Husband and wife wanting to know (or remember) what commitment looks like in real terms (even when it gets messy)
- Human who has gone through something hard or horrible
- Leader wanting to know the secrets to building trust
- Person who has made a mistake and wonders how to make it right
- Person who feels stuck, looking for actionable ways to move forward
- Person who wonders what values look like in action

- Person who has sacrificed (and wonders if they made a difference)

I am sure I have left out some groups, but this list pretty much covers all of us. Everyone who reads this book will find something that resonates.

This is a mentoring story. Through it, many will be impacted by Joel's father's life and his example. I was truly inspired by the man he was and how he quietly and powerfully lived his values. I am deeply grateful for his service. The stories contained in this book are authentic. I believe you, the reader, will relate to them easily. I know I did. Joel has created 'shared-human space' with this book.

In addition to that shared-human space, Joel gives us a powerful process for 'unpacking' horrific events. It's how we tell the story (to ourselves and others) that will ultimately determine how we move forward. How we frame those events -- what we pull from those experiences -- will shape who we become in the future.

The example Joel shares when speaking about being both divorced AND committed is powerful. It is unusual in our society to remain committed to family when a marriage ends in divorce, and yet it is so important for the future that we do this.

Finally, I love how this book honors the author's father. I pray blessings over this work. May it reach and touch every life God intended.

Dondi Scumaci

Introduction

This book is about servant leadership and how that will change every area of your life. Because I am a Christian, the book also contains many references to Christianity, Jesus, and the Bible. The reason for this is simple: Christ was the perfect servant-leader and thus the ultimate example of this leadership style.

This book was originally written from a non-religious standpoint, but after talking with a close friend and mentor who had read the draft, I was convinced that the book I had written was not the book that I should have written. Thus, after some significant re-writes in every chapter, this is the final product. I believe it is much better than it was, even if being open about my faith means that fewer people will read the book. The goal of this project is to present solid leadership principles, founded in Scripture, presented with truth and love.

Having said that, I strongly believe in the principles in this book, and I believe that they apply equally well in many different settings: the home, the workplace, academia, etc. I also believe that the principles and action steps will be beneficial to everyone, whether you are a believer in Jesus or not.

If you are reading this and you are a believer, thank you! I appreciate your time, and I'm honored that you found my book worthy of being read. I hope that the book encourages, inspires, and challenges you.

If you are reading this and you are not a believer, thank you! I appreciate your time even more, and I'm honored that you would take the time to read a book even if you disagree with some of the things in it. I hope it also encourages, inspires, and challenges you.

Finally, if you are looking for some solid principles without wanting to read through some of the various stories that illustrate the principles, I would encourage you to read the book slightly differently: first, read the beginning section of each chapter; next, read through the various sub-headings in each chapter as well as anything in bold print or italics; and third, read and go through the action steps at the end of each chapter. For a review of the major principles, you can immediately go to the back of the book and see the list there.

Thank you again, dear reader, for taking the time to go through *Inverted Leadership*, and I hope that reading the book is able to help you as much as writing it has helped me. I'd love to hear from you, so please feel free to connect with me via social media or email. You can reach me at joel@speakerjoel.com, on Twitter(@RealLifeLeading),Facebook(facebook.com/reallifeleading), or LinkedIn (Joel Hawbaker). May God bless you wherever you are on your leadership journey, and may He reveal Himself to you more and more.

Joel Wesley Hawbaker, 6/4/18

P.S. If you enjoy the book, I'd be very grateful if you'd take a minute to leave a rating and review on Amazon. Thanks!

Chapter 1

Confident Humility: Leadership as Service and Art

"We are living to glorify God and to serve others with our abilities. We are living in the light of Christ's resurrection, and so are like the Israelites just after they were delivered from slavery in Egypt. We work because we may, not because we must." - Dr. Bill Davis, in *In All Things Christ Preeminent*

Part I: What Is Confident Humility?

In 21st century America, we are facing a crisis of leadership. For a variety of reasons, we are seeing public leadership failures on an unprecedented scale, from small-towns to Washington, D.C. Whether it's the growing divorce rate or Congressional government shutdowns, it seems that we have reached a point of crisis in our world, and the reason for that crisis is self-centered pride. We, as a human race, have become more self-focused than ever before, and as a result, we are failing in our task of leadership. So, if pride is the source of the problem, if a failure of leadership is the result, then what is the solution? How do we begin the task of putting things right?

Lead Others Better By Forgetting About Yourself

The answer is the same as it has been throughout history: by following the example of Jesus Christ. That is, through confident humility, servant leadership, and self-forgetfulness. Just as Jesus was both confident in the Father's love and humble enough to do the Father's will, as He was willing to serve those he was leading, and as He was willing to put aside his own desires for the sake of the Father's plan, so we must also be willing to follow that difficult path. It is the aim of this book to help us become better informed and better equipped to accomplish the difficult task lying before us, using wisdom from others who have gone before us as our primary guide.

My father is from a small farm town in Illinois called Paw Paw, with a population of less than 900 people. He was able to go to college at Illinois Wesleyan in the 1960s. A year after he graduated from college, he was drafted to serve in the Vietnam War. After that, he decided to make a career in the military, staying in the army for 20 years, eventually joining the 82nd Airborne, going through Ranger School, and winning numerous medals and commendations, including three Bronze Stars. He finally retired, having attained the rank of Lieutenant Colonel. Just before he retired, though, he was up for promotion to the rank of Colonel, which would have been a significant step up in rank, in pay, and in prestige. However, because Dad knew he was planning to retire, he withdrew his name from consideration for the promotion.

I asked him about this later in his life, and I asked him why he chose to withdraw his name. Dad's answer was an excellent example of what will be called Confident Humility. He simply said, "Because I don't need to know." Dad then went on to explain how, though he was curious if he would have been considered worthy of this major promotion, ultimately waiting to see if he got promoted would have been counter-productive to the Army and thus to the country. He admitted it would have been fun to wait and see if he got the promotion. But he also knew that by waiting to be promoted only to then immediately retire from the military would have benefited only himself. Therefore, he chose to go ahead and retire without ever finding out about that promotion. He just didn't need to know.

That idea of not needing to know is exactly what this entire book is about: this concept of Confident Humility, leading others and serving others without focusing on yourself. It is self-belief that is used in the service of other people. This idea is upside down and backwards, entirely counter-cultural because it is based on what is eternal rather than what is temporal; it is based on Jesus rather than on what is good for us. We often measure success by how much we can accumulate, or how far and quickly we can get promoted--things that are self-focused and self-centered. As a result of that, we have come to a point where there is a gap between what success and leadership *are* and what they *ought* to be. This book is an attempt to begin correcting that misunderstanding by helping people rethink leadership based on an eternal perspective, beginning with the concept of Confident Humility.

Confidence vs. Pride

The first thing we have to do is to understand some basic terminology, specifically the difference between confidence and pride. *Webster's New Collegiate Dictionary* defines confidence as "faith or trust; a feeling or consciousness of one's powers or of reliance on one's circumstances; the quality or state of being certain." Confidence, then, is simply self-belief; it is knowing that you're good at something. That is an excellent quality to have as an athlete, a parent, an employee, or a boss. As a coach, I want my high school soccer players to be confident in their abilities. As a father, I want both of my daughters to be confident in who they are and who they were created to be. Because we are God's creations, we can have confidence in who He says we are: image-bearers of Himself to the world around us. All people, believers and non-believers alike, are God's image-bearers, and this should give us all the confidence we need to accomplish God's desire in the world.

How is this confidence different than pride? Though they might seem the same, the key difference is that confidence of the type described above is entirely dependent on who God is, while pride is much more focused on what we think ourselves to be. Again appealing to *Webster's New Collegiate Dictionary,* pride is defined as "inordinate self-esteem." It is a belief in yourself that goes beyond your abilities, and crucially, pride is ultimately competitive, according to C.S. Lewis. He tells us that pride is not just knowing that you are good at something. Rather, pride is believing that you are better than someone else; and because pride is ultimately competitive, it is also much more destructive. It's not just knowing that you are smart; pride feels the need to prove and show that you are smarter than someone else. Again, C.S. Lewis tells us that pride does not take pleasure in having money; rather, it only takes pleasure in having more money than others. Lewis even goes so far as to state, "It was through Pride that the devil became the devil...it is the complete anti-God state of mind" (from *Mere Christianity*). Thus, there is a huge difference between pride and confidence. Confidence is used to build others up using whatever skills and intelligence you have; pride is used to put and hold others down.

When we understand confidence in that way, we see the large difference between it and the pride that permeates so much of our culture. Another way to see it is that the difference between confidence and pride is a teacher who knows they are a good teacher based on seeing their students' growth, compared to a teacher who constantly worries about whether they are better than other teachers or are going to be shown up by their students. It has been said that, "A good teacher eventually makes themselves obsolete to their students." The suggestion there is that if teachers are doing what we are supposed to, eventually our students become self-sufficient learners, and we are no longer necessary to that set of students. Only confident teachers can do this; a prideful teacher will never do this because he is not willing to be unneeded.

Humility vs. False Humility

Humility is often misunderstood; it may even be one of the most misunderstood words in the English language. Many people think that humility is pretending that you're not as good at something as you actually are; they contrast pride--believing too much in yourself--with humility, and thus it becomes not believing enough in yourself. Again, from *Webster's New Collegiate Dictionary*, humility is "the quality or state of being humble." Even the dictionary seems determined to be unhelpful in defining the term! Humble is defined as "not proud or haughty; not arrogant or assertive." Well, that's a bit better, though only telling us what humble is NOT still doesn't help us understand what humble or humility IS. This also causes Confident Humility to seem like a paradox: if you believe you're good at something (confidence), how can you also believe you're not very good at it (humility misunderstood)? Fortunately, that is not at all what humility is.

C. S. Lewis tells us that humility is not smart people feigning stupidity or attractive people pretending that they are ugly or good athletes trying to believe that they really are not very good. Can you imagine someone asking Michael Jordan (or, for you younger readers Lebron James, Kobe Bryant, or Steph Curry) if he was a good basketball player, and him replying, "Well, I mean, I guess I'm ok. I wasn't really better than anyone else." Can you imagine how absurd it would be for someone to ask Leonardo da Vinci if he was a good artist and have him reply, "Well, I was adequate but not outstanding." One final absurdity: can anyone truly imagine Mother Teresa saying, in response to questions about the effectiveness of her ministry, "I wasn't actually very helpful to anyone."

That seems to be what we think of when we think of someone being humble or modest, and yet, when you see it like that, the response is absurd! Of course, those people were amazing! Why should they say or pretend otherwise? Because we misunderstand pride and because we misunderstand humility. Due to these misunderstandings, we learn from a young age that stating we are good at something sounds prideful or boastful, when in reality it might simply be stating a fact. That, CSL says, is false humility, which is really just dishonesty. Rather, *"Humility is not thinking less of yourself. Humility is thinking of yourself less."* Humility is nothing more than focusing on other people rather than focusing on yourself.

When you think of humility, you ought to think of people like Dr. Martin Luther King, Jr., who spent his adult life in service of others and in pursuit of correcting wrongs in the world, regardless of the dangers of his work to himself and his family. Or think of Mohandas Gandhi, who was one of the inspirations for Dr. Martin Luther King's nonviolent protests and civil disobedience. Or think of Mother Teresa who spent her life serving the poor. If those people feel a bit far-removed, a bit on a pedestal and unrealistic for most of us to aim for, then consider others closer to home, such as parents, especially stay-at-home parents. There are no paychecks for child-rearing, there aren't really any promotions, and as any parent will tell you, the effects of parenting on one's bank account are overwhelmingly negative. So why do parents do what they do? Because they are focused not on themselves but rather on helping their children. That's one way to see what humility is.

Putting it together--what is Confident Humility?

Confident Humility is others-centered servant leader-ship; it is self-belief used in the service of others. It is taking the gifts and talents that God has blessed you with and using them to influence other people in a positive way, to help them become better versions of themselves. That's what this whole book is about, because Confident Humility has the power to transform every relationship, every leadership role, every area of your life. Remember the story about my dad from the first page? That is what Confident Humility looks like: it is using your talents to the utmost to serve and help other people, without caring who gets the credit and without waiting for recognition. When we understand leadership in light of the Gospel, it causes us to view it in an inverted way, upside down, with Christ and other people as the focus. And this will change everything about the way we lead and relate to others.

Part II: Values And Character.

Former U.S. President Jimmy Carter wrote a book called *Our Endangered Values* back in 2005, and my dad gave me this book as a gift for Christmas not long after that. In the book, President Carter talks about the importance of values, not just at the personal level but at the societal level. Specifically he talks about the importance of values in America, and I believe he had very important things to say, because values shape who we are, they shape our decision making, and the values individuals hold also then shape the values of our society. So now that we understand the basic idea of Confident Humility, we next need to talk about values and character and why they are important to leaders.

In the ancient and medieval world, when discussing values, there was a focus on what were called the Four Cardinal Virtues. They were called 'cardinal' not because of the bird or the position in certain church hierarchies, but because the word for *cardinal* comes from a word that refers to a hinge in a door; that is, these four values are the four on which all other values turn or rest. These four values are justice, temperance, prudence, and fortitude, and many different authors have written extensively about these virtues and how they shape a person's life. I mention them here because the values we hold shape our personal character. Put differently: what we believe shapes who we are and what we do. Honesty, integrity, and hard work are also aspects of character and thus of Confident Humility.

Today, we are seeing a crisis of leadership because we as a society have fallen away from these traditional values. Even within the Church (I capitalize it here to refer to the eternal body of believers, not just to our various local assemblies) it has become not only normal but expected to be disrespectful to people with whom we disagree. It has become normal to blame others instead of accepting responsibility for the consequences of our choices. So, two of the major focuses of Confident Humility are "Give and Take." That is, we should always GIVE respect, even to people with whom we disagree. And we should always TAKE responsibility for our choices and their consequences, even if it costs us in the short-term. This is what Christ did, and it is what we are called to do as well.

Can you imagine, especially after the 2016 US Presidential election, a presidential debate that was characterized by true respect between the various candidates, rather than the passive-aggressive insults and insinuations among the candidates (even in the same party)? Can you imagine a politician ever giving a news conference to apologize for something *before* a scandal has broken, or in order to simply take responsibility for something that was done which he or she has now changed their mind about? Today it seems the only time people take responsibility for negative choices is when they have been outed and are now trying to save their reputation. As the old saying goes, "Success has many parents, but failure is an orphan."

Again, Confident Humility turns that on its head, saying that our first job is to give respect to other people while taking responsibility for our choices and our actions. Confident Humility focuses on serving other people, creating good relationships between leader and audience, and on building other people up regardless of who gets the credit for accomplishments. When my wife and I got married, her father said something at our wedding about love that I believe also is very applicable in this context. He said, "Love is choosing someone else's ultimate good over your own." I believe this is absolutely how leaders ought to operate: by choosing the ultimate good of other people over themselves. The greatest example of this is Jesus, who through love for us and a desire to do the Father's will, gave Himself up for us on the cross.

My job as a teacher and a parent is not to make myself look good or try to win awards for my teaching and parenting. My job is to educate my students and my daughters, teaching them values and skills that will help them to leave my classroom and home as better people than they were when they came in. It's to help them learn to love other people, to be respectful of others, and to then pass on what they have learned by serving others in turn.

Remember the Golden Rule from your youth? "Treat others the way you would want to be treated." Or, for those who prefer the slightly more archaic language, "Do unto others as you would have them do unto you." The same applies to leadership: "Lead others the way you would want to be led." Would you want to be led by someone with good character, solid values, and a kind heart? Do you want to be led by someone who is pursuing God's will rather than his or her own gain? Then we need to strive to be that person in our own leadership as well.

A quick note here: this does *not* mean that you have to be perfect. Good character does not mean that you will not ever make mistakes (as most of us know, since we have made mistakes of varying sizes throughout our lives). It *does* mean, though, that when we mess up we take responsibility for our actions and then we do the best we can to fix what we have broken both in terms of relationships and other consequences. It also means that we have a duty to learn from our mistakes and move forward, armed with new knowledge and experiences that we can apply to help us avoid making similar mistakes in the future.

One of the many joys of the Gospel is the knowledge that, because of Christ, God does not hold our sin or our mistakes against us, and thus we also should not hold them against ourselves. This is a huge aspect of character: a continual striving for perfection, knowing it is unachievable, and doing the best we can anyway. Thus one of the larger components of the Golden Rule is continually recognizing ways that we have messed up and then seeking to learn from those mistakes and become better, while helping others to do the same.

Part III: What's The Big Deal? Benefits Of Confident Humility.

Imagine a world full of respectful, responsible, God-centered relationships. Perhaps the divorce rate would plummet; perhaps not. But in a more realistic way, imagine a world where parents, even if they decide to divorce, continued to be respectful toward each other and continued to take responsibility for putting their children first. Imagine a situation in which we have an entire society of leaders looking out not for themselves, their bank accounts, and their political parties, but rather are looking out for what God says is right and good and true. And then, imagine a society that, instead of uniting around common enemies (the "us vs. them" mentality that is so prevalent in politics, athletics, and even family life) chooses to unite around common values and around Jesus.

I live in Alabama, and as I'm writing this, it is college football season. For those of you that are not from around here, the single largest argument starter in Alabama in the fall has nothing to do with politics or religion. The largest argument starter from August to January is football: Alabama or Auburn. If you live in or around North Carolina, you see a similar dichotomy in college basketball concerning Duke and UNC. In politics the divide is clear between Democrats and Republicans. In society at large and even within the Church, throughout history there has been a "male vs. female" divide, with women getting short-changed in almost every society.

In my history classes, I repeat to my students a very common adage: "Nothing unites people like a common enemy." And in the South, the common enemy is either Auburn or Alabama; it's almost as if you don't have a choice. Even if a person doesn't really watch football, most people will have at least a nominal allegiance to one or the other of those two football programs. What is amazing is that people who otherwise do not get along at all--due to differences in politics, age, race, gender, socioeconomic backgrounds, or whatever--all of those things go out the window when uniting *against* people who cheer for the other team. Alabama fans will get along with each other if for no other reason than to unite against Auburn fans, and Auburn fans are every bit as prone to this as well. This may seem like a silly example, but if you follow the news in Alabama, you will see that almost every year at least one person is shot over post-Iron Bowl (the nickname given to the annual Auburn-Alabama game) arguments.

This is simply a symptom of a larger problem: we live in a broken and fallen world. Again, "Nothing unites people like a common enemy." This is seen in sports, politics, race relations, families, and every area of life, if we are honest with ourselves. I invite you to take a moment and reflect on the areas in your life where this is most clearly seen. And then I want you to take a moment and try to imagine a world where people instead unite around common values and where people extend each other the same type of grace and mercy that has been extended to us through the life, death, and resurrection of Jesus.

Imagine a world where people of all different backgrounds, races, creeds, and political affiliations united around a desire to help others, instead of bad-mouthing people who want to help differently (e.g. competing political groups). Imagine a world where families united around a desire to love each other, rather than uniting against "the world outside." Imagine a team uniting around a set of common values and goals, instead of uniting to "crush our opponents." And then, if you can imagine such a world, let us move forward into making that into reality.

My daughters love the Harry Potter series (both the books and the movies), and in *Harry Potter and the Order of the Phoenix*, Harry is teaching other students certain skills and spells that they should be learning in class but are not, skills that they need in order to protect themselves from the dangers lurking outside the protective walls of their castle-school. In this particular scene, Harry says, "Think of it this way; every great wizard in history has started out as nothing more than what we are now, students. If they can do it, why not us?" Same idea here, dear readers. Dr. Martin Luther King, Jr., Gandhi, Mother Teresa, stay-at-home parents, or parents who work multiple jobs to make ends meet: every great leader throughout history had to begin somewhere. If they can become great leaders, why not us? Let us become what we want to see: great leaders, great family members, great influencers, creators of better relationships and a better society by trying to lead in the way that Jesus led. Begin today, wherever you are. I invite you to consider Confident Humility as a step in this direction. In doing so, we will look at three major themes of Confident Humility: 1) Lead Where You Are; 2) Be the First; 3) Lead Through Learning. As we explore these themes, I hope you will see the tremendous potential of Confident Humility as we rethink leadership and consider ways in which we can better serve and thus impact other people.

"Be the change you want to see in the world." - Mohandas Gandhi

Questions to Consider

1. What specific leadership gifts has God given you and how have you used them to serve others in the past?

2. What are areas of potential pride in your life, and how can you seek to mitigate that?

3. What aspects of Confident Humility do you need to focus on right now, and who can you ask to help you?

Action Step:

Choose one of the three aspects of Confident Humility and write down three ideas about how you can grow in that area.

Chapter 2

CEOs or Youth Soccer Coaches: Lead Where You Are

Part I: Rethinking Leadership.

Confident Humility is all about rethinking leadership, understanding it differently in order to transform how we lead and why we lead. Here, we're going to examine the first principle of Confident Humility: **LEAD WHERE YOU ARE**.

For four years, I had a girl named Lou* on the high school soccer team that I coach. Lou was a great teammate and athlete, willing to play anywhere on the field that I needed her to and work hard whenever she was on the field. As a junior, she was a key player on a very good team--this group lost only one game all year: the state championship game. In fact, Lou scored our only goal in the state championship game, our school's first appearance there in soccer, as we lost 4-1. In part because of our team's success that year, Lou came back very excited about playing again her senior year, even though her real love and focus was on volleyball. However, some time before Lou's senior soccer season, her mother was diagnosed with breast cancer, and everything changed. Lou's dad travels a lot for his job, often gone for much of the month. She also has an older brother who is away at college and a younger brother who has special needs, and her mother was typically responsible for the day-to-day running of the household.

However, when Lou's mom was diagnosed with cancer, their whole world changed drastically and instantly. Lou's senior year of high school went from being one in which she had some responsibility (as all student-athletes do) to one in which she had more responsibility than most girls her age. She now was tasked with helping take care of her younger brother and her mom, especially in those weeks when her father had to travel. All of this was in addition to keeping up her grades so that she could graduate and hopefully get scholarships for college the next year. Because of these things, she came to me before our soccer season started and said, "Coach, I really want to play, but I know I can't make it to practice every day. Sometimes I'm going to have to go pick up my brother because my mom will be doing chemotherapy or recovering from a recent treatment, and so I just can't make it every day. I really want to play. What do I need to do?" Like few young people I have known, and very much in the manner of Christ, Lou immediately began putting the needs of others before her own needs and desires.

I am very glad to have had the opportunity to tell her, "Lou, you do whatever you need to in order to take care of your family. We would love to have you at practice every day, but I agree that it is not realistic to expect you to do that, nor would it be possible. So, take care of your family, and whenever you can be here, we'll be glad to have you." Lou had to step up at age eighteen and become a leader in her family and home, due to life circumstances beyond her control.

Here's the truth about leadership: most of us will not be CEOs of multinational corporations with thousands of employees in our charge; most of us won't be college presidents, responsible for dozens or hundreds of faculty members and hundreds or even thousands of students. Most of us will never be military commanders with soldiers' lives in our hands; we are unlikely to be professional sports coaches, responsible for managing multi-millionaire athletes and some of their egos. But many of us will be parents, Sunday school teachers, or volunteers in local civic groups. We will be youth soccer coaches, organizers of small drama groups, or helpers at local animal or homeless shelters. Though our audience or organizations may be smaller, we will all be leaders in various ways because we have been called by God to further the ends of His kingdom while we are here on earth. The key is to remember: *just because the setting and audience size are smaller, this does not mean that our leadership matters any less. In fact, the smaller our setting and audience, the more important the leadership due to the larger potential impact we can have on each individual within our audience or organization.* Think of the person that has impacted your life the most: was it a celebrity or athlete or CEO? For most of us, the person who impacted us the most is someone we spent significant time with in a smaller setting: a teacher, a coach, a youth pastor, a caring adult, or someone similar.

I have an immediate family of four: myself, my wife, and our two daughters. I also have classes averaging twenty students per class, and I have an average of thirty soccer players in my program at any given time. The amount of influence I can have on my wife and daughters far outweighs the influence I can have over each student or soccer player that I have. The smaller the organization, the more influence and impact the leader can have. Thus, the first principle of Confident Humility, LEAD WHERE YOU ARE, means this: **every role is either a leadership role or preparation for a future leadership role, so begin leading wherever you are right now.**

We need to make sure we remember what leadership is: I define leadership as **the art of positively influencing others to help them become better versions of themselves.** Leadership is not simply exercising authority or managing a bottom line. Our job as leaders is to be a positive influencer and a value teacher, helping others to become better people and better at whatever roles they are in. My job as a parent is to help my kids eventually become responsible adults who love the Lord; my job as a teacher is to help my students to become lifelong learners and servants of Christ; my job as a coach is to help my players see the Gospel and thus become better people through how we play the game of soccer. And this is true of any leadership roles you find yourself in as well: your job is to positively influence and impact the people around you to help them become better versions of themselves. Leadership is not about titles, it's not about paychecks, it's not about prestige. It is about serving other people as value-creators and teachers so that they can become more like Christ.

Part II: Leaders Are Value-Creators.

Good leaders, Godly leaders, are going to teach values to their audience and help them to apply those values throughout their organizations and lives. There's a great book called *The West Point Way of Leadership* by (Ret.) Colonel Larry R. Donnithorne. In that book, the author explains that every aspect of leadership taught at West Point begins with character training, just as we discussed in chapter one. Thus, good leaders are going to pass on the values of their organization to their audience, whether those are the Four Cardinal Virtues or values such as service, selflessness, honesty, integrity, or any other values the organization stands for. Again, one major aspect of leadership is passing on values.

As parents, we talk about wanting to help our children become good people and responsible adults. Thus, our children need to know what our family stands for, and so in our home we actually have a motto that summarizes our family's values in a brief, three-word phrase: "Truth and love." Because we are a bit nerdy, we also like to use the Latin translation, "Veritas et amor." This helps us remember that our job as parents is to show our children how "truth and love" apply in every role and situation they will encounter in their lifetimes. We believe that the values of "truth and love" reflect the heart of Christ and thus should be at the center of everything we do and everything we are.

In addition to teaching values, a good leader is also going to show how each role within an organization has value. Each role matters and contributes to the successful functioning of the organization. When I was younger, I played soccer for Covenant College. Despite what my ego wants me to say, the truth is that I was not as good of a player as most of my teammates. In fact, I only played in a few games my freshman year, but one of my strengths was my ability to work hard and to encourage my teammates, both in practice and during games. As the season went on, and as I realized my role was less about playing in games and more about helping my teammates become better, that is where I focused my time and energy.

During games I would get water for the players coming off the field, I would encourage them, and I would try to engage them in conversation that would help them understand what was happening on the field better (which, coincidentally, also helped me understand things better as well). In practice, I would work hard and try to do whatever I could to challenge the starting players, often playing in multiple positions in the same practice simply to match up with different players that needed work. As with the title character in the classic football movie *Rudy*, my job was to make the good players work hard in practice so that they would be better on game day.

As a result of my efforts, about halfway through my freshman year, my coach gave me a semi-mocking title, naming me "Bench Captain" for that season. I was not sure if I should be insulted or not at this title, and I eventually came to the conclusion that I probably should have been at least mildly insulted by this. On the other hand, I have since realized that whether it was intended to be insulting or not, he was acknowledging that I was providing leadership in a way that no one else on the team was. So if my job was to encourage players while I was on the bench, that had to be ok. We were nationally ranked in the NAIA Top 25 for much of that season, and most players or coaches that have been a part of a high-level team recognize the value of those types of role players. It wasn't glamorous, and it certainly wasn't what I had imagined my role would be when I pursued my dream of playing college soccer; but it was the role that God had called me to and the role that the coach assigned me to, and thus it was a role that needed to be fulfilled to the best of my ability.

If your job in an organization is to support others and help them perform their jobs better, excellent: that is leadership. Obviously, that was not what I had dreamed of as a middle school soccer player. But it was the reality of the situation I was in, and therefore it became the focus of my efforts. I will not lie and say that I enjoyed every moment of it. But looking back, I can honestly say that the coach was right not to play me more, and by doing my utmost to fulfill that role, I know that God was at work teaching me humility and reinforcing the value of hard work in my life.

My father-in-law has a master's degree in business administration from the University of Alabama-Birmingham, and he recounts something that one of his management professors taught him: "Management is getting other people to do what you want because they want to do it." I think this is an excellent way of thinking about management as one aspect of leadership: when leaders act as value-creators, our audience will come to a place in which they do what needs to be done because they want to do it, not because they have to be bribed or threatened or guilt-tripped into doing it. One of the major ways we do that is by helping people to see the value in their individual roles and how those roles contribute to the overall success of the group or organization. Within the body of Christ, there are many roles; Paul compares these to how the body has many members each with a different function. When we remember that we, despite our varying roles, are part of the body of Christ, we can recognize that our efforts are not useless or wasted no matter how unglamorous they may appear to the world outside.

Part III: Goal-Setting--Why It Matters And What Our Goals Reveal.

Another crucial aspect of LEAD WHERE YOU ARE is setting goals for the group or organization. Within every role, if we are to be successful, we have to have a clear idea of what we are trying to accomplish. We have to know what our goals are. There is a saying that is often heard around various organizations, stating, "If you aim at nothing, you will hit it every time." Thus we need to aim at something, to set goals and make sure that they are specific, measurable, and attainable. Many different authors have written about goal-setting and why most people fail to reach their goals, and one of the common reasons is because many goals are not clearly defined. Think of how many New Year's resolutions revolving around diet and exercise are made and not kept every single year. Goals that are vague, or have no time frame component, or that are unrealistic--these are really just setting your organization up for failure and the accompanying discouragement that inevitably follows. As Christians, we should have one goal always at the forefront of our minds: when we have crossed into eternity, to hear God say to us, "Well done, good and faithful servant." That should be the ultimate goal that shapes our every decision in this life.

The reason this matters is because the goals we are pursuing shape our decisions, our outcomes, and most importantly, they shape our reactions to our outcomes especially if we fail to reach our earthly goals. In addition to coaching my high school team, I have also spent a number of years coaching my daughters' youth soccer teams. Every year, at my preseason parent meeting, I tell players and parents the targets for the upcoming season. These are always the same, and they are very simple:

1. I want the players to have fun, because if they have fun, they will want to keep playing (and really, it is a game, so let's enjoy it!), and so the players are happy;

2. I want the players to learn something new and/or improve at something, every practice and every game, because if they learn something or improve at something each time we are together, I will be happy and they will become better players; and

3. I want the players to work hard and go home tired from every practice and game because if they do this, then their parents will be happy!

   If you notice, nowhere in there did I mention winning games or scoring a certain amount of goals or competing for championships or trophies because when I am coaching six- to twelve-year-olds, the emphasis should not be on winning games. If you win every game as a ten-year-old but you did not actually improve as a player, you wasted that season of development. Now, to be clear, I was ultra-competitive--as a kid, I broke a number of video game controllers, and as a young adult my family did not enjoy playing games with me due to my poor attitude whenever I lost. So when I coach youth soccer I want to win. But because these are younger players the emphasis should be on teaching values through soccer, on development and character and life lessons. If we become better people and we become better soccer players, we will also win a lot of games along the way. In the excellent book *The Messiah Method* by Michael Zigarelli, the author discusses how this idea of pursuing excellence in Christ is at the core of the men's and women's soccer programs at Messiah College. As a result of this pursuit of Christ, this program has become the winningest college soccer program in America, not by focusing on winning but by focusing on glorifying God every day in all that they do. Think about it: if every player is getting better every practice and game, we are also getting better as a team, and that will translate to winning. But winning is not the focus; it is simply a by-product of our pursuit of the things of Christ.

One of the best ways to make sure that your organization reaches your goals is to write them down and post them somewhere that they will be seen on a regular basis. Again, you can find lots of great books about goal-setting and reaching your goals (from *The Power of Focus* by Canfield, Hansen, and Hewitt to *Finish: Give Yourself the Gift of Done* by Jon Acuff), and I strongly recommend that you pick up the two mentioned here. When I took over the high school soccer program that I currently oversee five years ago, the program had never won an area championship or a playoff game. So after my first season there (which ended with us losing our first-round playoff game in overtime, as close as we had ever gotten to winning one), we set new goals.

Remember, this is a high school team, so there is more of an emphasis on winning, though it is not our primary aim. In fact, our motto is "Walk worthy," a phrase taken directly from Paul's admonition in Ephesians chapter four to "walk in a manner worthy of the calling to which you have been called." In direct imitation of Messiah College, our program is consciously focused on pursuing Christ through soccer, and thus winning also becomes a bi-product of our efforts. We hope to win, and thus we do also set goals that talk about soccer-specific accomplishments. Our goals for that season included winning a certain percentage of our games, winning an area title, and winning our first-ever playoff game. After deciding on our goals, we wrote them down on a giant poster and put it up in our locker room. As the season went on, we put a check-mark next to each goal as it was reached. We put check marks next to scoring a certain amount, to winning a certain amount of games, to giving up less than a certain amount of goals to our opponents, and eventually we got to put a check next to winning our first area title. As this continued, the players began to look forward to accomplishing each new goal, because they saw a reminder everyday of what we had accomplished and what was still left to be done. It was incredible to see how much the players enjoyed putting a check mark up as the season continued!

Keep in mind, these are high school kids with all the normal concerns, complications, and cares of being in high school. This was not a fancy set up, either: it was a large, plain white poster with goals written on it in black permanent marker by one of the players whose handwriting is much better than mine. But because they saw those goals every day, they knew what we were trying to accomplish that year. Our overall goal was to become the best soccer team in the school's history. The way we set about doing that was by focusing on achieving these smaller, more measurable goals along the way. After the season, when we accomplished everything we had set out to do, we took the poster down, but we kept it in the locker room, and it is still there as a reminder of what we did that season. This helps the girls that played that year remember what it was like, and it encourages the newer players to set and achieve similar goals each new season.

The last part about goal-setting that is crucial to our understanding of leadership and values is that our goals reveal certain things about ourselves. Our goals reveal whether we mean what we say or whether we are just paying lip-service to something. As a teacher, I have heard many parents say that they want their children, my students, to be good at school, or get good grades, or learn. But often these parents' actions revealed that they didn't really want these things because when a student's grades went south, instead of asking the student what the problem was, parents instead came to me and ask why the student was struggling. On one hand this makes sense: I'm the teacher, so perhaps I have insight into the drop-in grades. On the other hand, it also reveals that often the parent also held me responsible for the grades, rather than the student being responsible for his/her grades. Some parents were less interested in what and how their child is learning; what they really were interested in is whether or not that child has a certain number in a grade book, regardless of what has or has not been learned. Thankfully, the vast majority of the parents whose children I have taught were not of this mindset, and it is also a good reminder to me to think about my own mindset in terms of my daughters' grades. In our context of leadership, it is important to be very clear what our true goals are and then be sure that our actions support our words.

The same issue exists in coaching youth soccer teams: if I tell the parents that my focus is on fun and learning, and yet during the games I yell at referees and players as if lives were at stake, then what I have revealed is that my true commitment is to winning games, not developing players and people through soccer. Thus, as leaders, we need to make sure that both the goals we set and *the way in which we approach those goals* are consistent with the values that we aspire to. Our goals and our decision-making as we try to achieve those goals say something about us: what we value and what we say we value may not be as consistent as we think. This is why it is important to write our goals down, and this is why it is important to make sure that we are doing what we say we are trying to do. If we as leaders begin to stray from our values and goals, we will be called out; and we need to have the humility to admit our mistakes and then reorient ourselves to our stated goals.

In addition to this, our goals do not just shape our outcomes; they also shape our reactions to our outcomes, whether we reach our goals or not. If my goal is to help my soccer players become better people, and we do not win a single game, then I may not be happy about losing but I can keep my eye on the bigger goal of helping these players develop into responsible adults. If we have learned and grown and improved, then losing is still not fun, but it is kept in its proper context and thus does not mean that I have to be distraught each time we lose nor do we have to consider the season as wasted. However, if we win soccer games by cheating or with poor attitudes, that reveals that I am more interested in winning than I am in helping develop players into better people. That would be poor leadership, poor service, and a poor reflection on our Creator.

If I am so committed to winning that we are willing to sacrifice our stated values for the sake of winning, then I am doing my players a disservice. The same is true in any business, team, or organization: we must remain committed to our values, even if that means we do not 'win' as often as we might prefer. Focus on your goals, make sure those goals are aligned with your values, and when you do those things, you will also notice that how you define success and failure will change. Success now becomes about reaching the full potential of your organization, and when each member sees their roles as valuable, the entire organization will improve, and the results will follow.

What we do, the goals we set, the way we approach those goals, and the way we react to our outcomes are all important aspects of LEAD WHERE YOU ARE. Just in case you were curious, my soccer player Lou that you met at the beginning of the chapter had an excellent senior year: she started many of our games, played numerous positions, and she even scored the game-winning goal in our team's first round playoff game that year! The game was against one of our rivals, she scored a beautiful goal, and we eventually made it all the way to the state championship game for the second year in a row. Perhaps the most fun part was that when she scored that goal, her mom (now cancer free!) was there and was recording the play on her phone, and we have shared it on our soccer team's website so that we can go back and rewatch it over and over again. Not every story has such a great and happy ending, but I am thrilled that Lou's did. Since then, she has gone to college and is doing extremely well. She has grown as a person and as a leader, and she started by following the first principle of Confident Humility: LEAD WHERE YOU ARE.

"You don't need a title to be a leader." - Unknown

Questions to Consider

1. In your opinion, how does leadership reflect the Gospel? How have you seen this done well, and how have you seen it done poorly? What can you learn from each?

2. What are the stated values of your organization? How consistently do the actions of your group line up with the stated values? How can you improve this?

3. What are some of your goals for leadership, and how can you accomplish them?

Action Step:

Write down one way in which you can better align your actions with your values.

Chapter 3

The Virgin Queen and the Little Corsican: Impact or Success?

In leadership, one of the key components that must be discussed is this: what is the purpose of your organization or group? Is it to achieve success, however that may be defined? Or is it to make an impact on those around you? As Christians, we must recognize this distinction between success and impact as of crucial importance to our leadership. Our role in the world is to further the ends of Christ's kingdom, and we begin by recognizing that this may not involve 'success' as defined by the world, but it will certainly involve making an impact on those around us for the Gospel.

Part I: Immediate Success Or Lasting Impact?

Queen Elizabeth I of England is known as the Virgin Queen because in a historical age dominated by men, especially male monarchs, she ruled England for over half a century, unwed. In fact, our state of Virginia is named for her, since the first attempt at English colonization there occurred during her reign--the Lost Colony of Roanoke, founded in 1587. Her reign in England is known as a time of political stability and a time when religious tolerance and peace was finally achieved after decades of bloodshed caused by the Protestant Reformation and the tumultuous reigns of King Henry VIII, his son Edward, and Elizabeth's older half-sister, the infamous Bloody Mary. Queen Elizabeth is known for surviving around two dozen assassination attempts, mainly believed to have been instigated by the Catholic rulers of Spain and the Vatican, and she is also known for establishing England as the dominant Protestant power in Europe.

By the time of her reign, the Protestant Reformation had spread throughout much of Europe, and religious wars were in full swing all over the continent. Because she was a woman, because England was growing in power, and because most of Europe was still Catholic, she was a target for both assassination and conquest attempts, whether marital or political. This is most clearly seen in the efforts of King Philip II of Spain, known in history as the Most Catholic King; he believed his role in history was to stop the growing spread of Protestantism and to reestablish Catholicism throughout Europe.

After having a marriage proposal to Elizabeth spurned, and after learning that many English pirates were capturing Spanish gold from the New World with the queen's blessing, Philip's Spanish Armada attempted to invade England in 1588. This invasion effort was beaten back, and Philip's fleet returned home with less than half of the ships and troops that had begun the invasion, in part thanks to a violent storm they encountered in the North Sea during their return voyage to Spain.

England was saved, Protestantism continued to grow there, Elizabeth continued to rule England, and the country grew in prestige and stability until her death. Thus, Queen Elizabeth I is an amazing example of a successful leader by any measurement, leading England for over fifty years while providing political stability, religious freedom, territorial expansion, and economic growth. And if all of that was not enough, a quick study of her life will also show you that in addition to being an amazingly successful leader, Elizabeth I was also rather eloquent. So, why is it that most people have not heard of or ever bothered to study her life? Is it perhaps that because, though she was successful, the direct impact of her rule is either less than we would expect or simply underappreciated?

Let's take another example: Napoleon Bonaparte, the Little Corsican who rose to power in France due to the French Revolution. Napoleon Bonaparte is the second most written about historical figure in world history, ranking only behind Jesus. Napoleon was originally from a family of minor nobility living on the island of Corsica--this, combined with his diminutive stature earned him the less-than-flattering nickname of "The Little Corsican". He was able to go to a French military academy on scholarship, and due to the outbreak of the French Revolution in 1789, he was able to quickly rise through the ranks of the French army, becoming a general in his early 20s. In 1799 he helped overthrow a provisional French government, and after becoming 'first consul' and then 'consul for life,' in 1804 he declared himself Emperor of the French.

From 1799-1815, Napoleon was the primary reason for wars throughout Europe, and some of these conflicts spread even farther, affecting much of the rest of the world. Napoleon needed money to fight his wars, and he wanted to make sure the British didn't seize French territory in North America, so he sold the Louisiana Purchase to the United States in 1803, effectively doubling the size of the country at that time. This also served to unintentionally encourage Americans to continue migrating and expanding westward across the continent. Back in Europe and in various colonies, his wars are known for furthering the cause of nationalism in the early 19th century as well as for spreading Enlightenment ideas and practices. The effects of the Napoleonic Wars on Europe, northern Africa (especially Egypt), Asia, and

North America are difficult to measure, but they are certainly still being felt, as in the example above about the Louisiana Purchase.

The irony of this situation is that while the effects of his wars are still evident, the hard truth about Napoleon is that, in the end, his armies lost badly in both Russia and in modern-day Belgium, and he was eventually exiled twice. Due to his disastrous Russian invasion in which he lost around half a million men in less than a year, he was eventually defeated and exiled for the first time in 1814, after the Allies invaded France and even captured Paris. The following year, after secretly escaping from the island of Elba, he re-entered France (more on this later), gathered a new army, and was then defeated by the British Lord Wellington at Waterloo and exiled again in 1815. This time, though, the British made sure he would not be able to escape, exiling him to the tiny island of St. Helena in the South Atlantic. They learned from his first return that, despite having been defeated, Napoleon still had enough followers and admirers to be dangerous should he ever return again.

Very few, if any, people in Europe were untouched by Napoleon's reign, though his reign was significantly shorter (and much less 'successful') than Elizabeth's. The point is this: Elizabeth is an amazing example of a successful monarch who ruled for over half a century. Napoleon was a much more impactful monarch, though his reign was significantly shorter and ended in multiple defeats. Napoleon's impact, especially via nationalism and its effects on the development of various European countries, continued long after his death. Nationalism, after all, was one of the main causes of World War I, which began a hundred years after Napoleon's first exile. So, for us, the question is this: what type of leader do we want to be? Do we want to be successful, or do we want to be impactful?

Just as a final look at success vs. impact, consider briefly the life of Christ. His earthly ministry lasted only around three years. He spent most of his time with twelve specific men, though often crowds did gather to hear him speak. He had neither money nor political power, and he was eventually arrested, tortured, and killed by the reigning powers of his day. And at the very end of his earthly life, even his closest followers deserted him. Yet, following the Resurrection, his apostles remained faithful, his message spread to the ends of the earth, and He set in motion a movement that has had tremendous effects in every nation on earth despite the hostility of people and governments. This should tell us that our focus should be on impacting the world for the Gospel through our leadership, rather than seeking earthly success in whatever our chosen areas of influence are.

Part II: The Danger Of Focusing On Success.

Webster's New Collegiate Dictionary defines impact as, "the force of impression of one thing on another." It is the degree to which one thing shapes another thing; in our situation, impact is the amount of influence or change a leader brings about in the lives of her audience. Success is defined as "a favorable termination of a venture." Few people would call Napoleon's reign a success, based on those definitions, though Elizabeth fits nicely into that explanation.

These two ideas of success and impact are not mutually exclusive, but they are also not the same thing. As a leader, you have to choose whether you are going to focus on having success or on having impact. The best solution would obviously be to do both, but at some point every leader has to choose which one is the ultimate aim of your leadership. As seen in chapter one, the way in which a leader defines success will greatly shape your priorities and your response to setbacks.

As a soccer coach, one of our goals is obviously to win games. At the high school varsity level, winning is certainly part of our mindset and one of the reasons we play. We want to be a successful team each season and thus create a successful program in the long run. The danger for leaders is that focusing only on success can cause you to compromise your values or your relationships. In the fall of 2016, I was coaching my younger daughter's youth soccer team, and her stepdad was my assistant coach. In our fourth game of the season, we had one set of parents become extremely angry at us for the way they felt we were unfairly treating and talking to their son. During the game, the parents came over behind the bench and made their feelings known to us while we were still trying to pay attention to what was happening on the field. We had to politely ask them to wait until the game was over so that we could adequately discuss their grievance while also not ignoring the kids that were playing.

These parents were upset because we took their son out of the game after he failed to do as he had been instructed, and as he came off the field, the way in which we spoke to him was harsher than what the parents felt was necessary. They were correct--we were louder and angrier with him than we had any right to be. In that particular moment, we had taken our eyes off our stated goals for that youth soccer team (fun, learning, make them tired) and instead we had become focused on winning that particular game. Yes, the player needed to come off the field and be corrected; but the manner in which we went about it was wrong, because we were more focused on short-term success than we were on making a positive long-term impact on that particular player and on our team as a whole.

Most adults can tell stories like that: parents, teachers, coaches, managers, etc., have all had moments in which we forgot about our long-term impact, instead focusing on short-term results or success. Focusing on success alone can cause us to compromise our relationships and our values. For more examples of this, simply check out the news and read about the ways in which various athletic programs are getting caught cheating in how they recruit players, or about companies getting caught short-changing their customers in order to enhance the company's bottom line. This happens when we get so focused on the aspect of success that we forget about the impact we are having both now and for eternity.

Now, a quick word of warning: don't hear what I am not saying. I am not saying that success is bad, nor am I saying that we should never concern ourselves with success at all. Of course, we should! We all want to be successful in whatever areas we choose to spend our time. I want to be the best father, husband, coach, teacher, writer, speaker, and dog-owner that I can possibly be. But what does it mean to be the 'best' I can be? Does that have to do with success or impact? Each of us has to decide how we define these things and remember: choosing not to consciously think about this is still making a decision about it. Choosing not to consider these things is a way of saying that you do not consider them worth your time and consideration.

If you are a student reading this, how do you define your success? By your grades, your overall GPA, or by how well prepared your education is helping you become for life after school or college? Is it by getting a certain standardized test score or whether or not you get into the school you are hoping to attend? Is it by expanding your knowledge and skill sets so that you are growing into a more informed, more able person than you were before? Remember, how you define success will not only shape what you do but it will also shape your response when you do not achieve all of your goals. Our ultimate aim as Christians and as leaders should be to further the Gospel in whatever context we are in. If we are doing that, then we will be making an impact that matters not just now, but for eternity.

Part III: Why Focusing On Impact Will Also Help You Be Successful.

Focusing on impact means concentrating your efforts on having the most positive influence or effect possible on the people in your audience, and this goes back to your values. Very few people would argue that all of Napoleon's impact on Europe was good: there was too much bloodshed, too many wars, too many negative consequences associated with his reign, both inside of France and outside. On the other hand, there are more than a dozen European countries that exist now that did not exist during Napoleon's day, and many of those countries owe their existence to the strength of nationalism that Napoleon's wars unintentionally set loose.

As a student, perhaps focusing on grades is a good thing. But I would argue that focusing on learning certain skill sets (reading, writing, thinking, social skills, problem solving, etc.) and then refining those skill sets is even more important than any number in someone's gradebook (mine included). That means that as a teacher I need to focus on teaching those skill sets, not just making sure that my students achieve a certain grade or standardized test score. I need to make sure that I am teaching certain values that will impact the students long after they leave my classroom. Similarly, if you are a parent, I encourage you to focus not on your child's occupational prospects for the future, but instead to focus on the type of person your child is becoming, regardless of their grades or future paycheck potential.

Perhaps one reason so few people choose to focus on impact rather than success is that it is often much harder to measure, and so people often focus on success out of a type of default. That is, because success involves goal-setting and thus goal-measuring, it is easier to focus on this aspect of leadership, at the expense of paying attention to the long-term impact. Impact is a much more nebulous concept, harder to measure, more difficult to truly gauge. However, impact is also more important because it is longer-lasting and ultimately more powerful. When we remember that all of our efforts are seen by God, and when we focus our efforts on pleasing God, then it also becomes easier to remember that even if we don't see certain results or levels of earthly success our efforts are not wasted.

Remember the soccer poster I told you about earlier? It was a lot of fun to check those boxes as we reached those goals, and that poster is still around the locker room as a reminder. But the truth is, those goals have been met and therefore are in the past and have no bearing on what we will accomplish in the future. The impact of those players on each other, the impact of them on our program, and whatever impact I have been able to have on them is yet to be seen. The impact of last year's players will certainly affect our upcoming season, but more importantly it will affect the players after they move on from high school. Will some of them become teachers or coaches? How will they use the lessons they have learned playing soccer when they head to college, when they start careers, or when they have families of their own? These things are almost impossible to measure, but they are also far more important than any on-field success we may have. I am thankful to be able to coach and teach at a school that is more interested in the long-term impact of our athletic programs than on short-term success. We want to win, but more importantly we want to impact student-athletes for the Gospel so that they can do the same when they leave our school.

Part IV: Go For Both, But Focus On Impact Because It Matters More And Lasts Longer.

The key here, as in every aspect of leadership that we will discuss, is to find the balance between focusing on impact and paying attention to success. Only focusing on being successful may allow you to do that in the short-term, but it does so at the risk of limiting your long-term impact. Focusing only on impact, however, will ironically limit both your success and your impact because without any success your impact will not be lasting. As a soccer coach, if we only ever talk about becoming better people and we never actually practice soccer or get any better, many of the life lessons will be lost because of the players' perception of me as a poor coach.

Do any of us really want to be part of a team or organization that cares nothing for success? Of course not! It feels like a waste of time and whatever effort we put forth. As a parent, if I only ever focusing on 'helping' my child by saving them from any and every difficult situation, I am really doing them a disservice in the long run by robbing them of the opportunity for personal growth through problem-solving. Such parenting slows the child's ability to become self-sufficient and responsible, because the parent is always there to fix whatever problem the child has. Thus, the child may be a success in the short-term, but the parent's long-term impact is limited or even unintentionally negative.

Again, the key is to find the balance between impact and success. When attempting to do this, always err on the side of service, of helping others, of living for the sake of the Gospel rather than for any earthly reward. In this context that means to err on the side of impacting others even if it may cost you short-term success. If you impact your audience in the right way while also doing the work necessary to achieve many of your stated goals, then success will follow. Looking back at Napoleon and Elizabeth, it is quite clear which of them was more successful and which had more impact. Both of them are great historical examples of leadership to learn from: in all of their complexity, any student can glean positive and negative lessons from each of them. The question is which kind of leader do you want to be? A leader who is successful, a leader who is impactful, or maybe a leader who is both?

In your life, think of teachers, coaches, pastors, parents, or other adults who had a lasting impact on you. Were they all the most successful in their fields? Perhaps. Without a doubt, they were at least somewhat successful, or their impact would likely not have been so strong. But I would argue that whoever popped into your mind spent more of their time trying to do what was right, trying to serve others, and trying to help others improve, rather than simply focusing on personal success.

Consider Napoleon one final time: after his first exile to Elba, he was able to pull off a daring escape from the island and return to France, gathering new followers everywhere he went. When the newly-installed French king heard of Napoleon's return, he sent out the army to capture Bonaparte before he could reach Paris. At one point, the army blocked the road Napoleon was traveling, and they ordered him to surrender. Instead of surrendering and despite being outnumbered, Napoleon walked in front of the army by himself, opened his coat to expose his chest to the weapons of those sent to arrest or kill him, and said to them, "Soldiers, if there is one among you who wants to kill his general, his Emperor, here I am." In that moment, rather than shooting or arresting him, the soldiers responded with cries of "Long live the Emperor!", and then they joined Napoleon in his march toward Paris. This is an amazing historical example of a ruler who had so impacted people that he could turn an entire army to his cause with a few words. Yet even so, Napoleon's impact is as nothing compared to that of Jesus. And while we may not have the same impact of Jesus or even Napoleon or Elizabeth I, we all make an impact every single day.

"You cannot get through a single day without having an impact on the world around you. What you do makes a difference, and you have to decide what kind of difference you want to make."

- Jane Goodall

Questions to Consider

1. **In what ways have you tended to focus too much on success in your leadership, and how can you correct that?**

2. **In what ways have you neglected focusing on impact, and how can you fix that?**

3. How does the Gospel inform this aspect of your leadership?

Action Step:

Take a few minutes to reflect on your various leadership roles and write down three ways that you can make a more positive impact on your immediate circle.

Chapter 4

Is Winning Arguments Even A Thing? Results or Relationships

In leadership, it is often easy to forget that our job is not simply to get or achieve a desired result. We get caught up in trying to accomplish a stated goal or task, and we lose focus on the relationships that make any achievement possible. We forget that people are eternal, while anything we do here on earth, unless done for the Lord, will simply pass away one day. This chapter discusses how to remember and retain a focus on relationships rather than on results.

Part I: Be The First.

I got married for the first time after my sophomore year at Covenant College. After graduating from Covenant with a degree in History, my young family--which now included a baby girl, born less than a month after I got my diploma--and I moved five hundred miles north so that I could take up a job as a teacher and soccer coach at Fayetteville Christian School in North Carolina. While in Fayetteville, we lived in a house owned by my in-laws, and for a while, my brother-in-law came to live with us. One day he witnessed what I now see as one of the most embarrassing leadership failures of my first marriage. My wife had loaded the dishwasher and was getting ready to run it, but before she did I decided to move some of the dishes around.

Perhaps some of you can identify with feeling like you are the only person in the house who knows how to properly load the dishwasher. Well, both my wife and I felt that way about ourselves. So after I moved the dishes around, she went back and replaced every one into the positions she had put them in originally. Then I went and sorted them again and stood back watching as she again rearranged this dishes. This went on for probably ten minutes, while tempers and words continued to get hotter and louder, all while my brother-in-law watched (probably trying not to laugh at our ridiculousness). It's been over a decade since that event, and I honestly do not know how it ended or in what way the dishes were arranged when the dishwasher finally got turned on. What I do know is that no matter who "won" that argument, the real loser in that moment was our relationship.

Have any of you won an argument with your spouse or significant other and still been happy about it ten minutes later? How about with a child, friend, or colleague? Perhaps sometimes, but I know what most often happens when I win an argument is that a relationship is also damaged. There are hurt feelings, there is resentment, and there is a strain in that relationship that did not need to be there. The reason this matters is because in leadership, *everything starts with relationships*, and so we need to take care of them. If you take care of relationships, the results will take care of themselves. And the most important relationship to take care of is your relationship with Jesus; all other relationships flow from there.

We've all heard the expression "Don't judge a book by its cover," but the reality is that we all judge others based on appearances. I first really came to understand this while taking a class for a teacher certification, and in an excellent book titled *The*

First Days of School, written by Dr. Harry K. Wong, I came across this great nugget: "As you are dressed, so shall you be perceived. And as you are perceived, so shall you be treated." Therefore, as a teacher, I need to dress professionally if I expect students and teachers to take me seriously; doubly so for me, since I lack what is called "a commanding presence." What I mean is that I stand at the amazing height of 5'3" tall, and so unless I make myself stand out, when I walk into a room I am often mistaken for one of the freshmen that I teach. And the same thing happens with my soccer teams.

The truth is that, even if you have just met someone, there is the beginning of a relationship since we subconsciously have formed some kind of initial judgment based on appearance, greeting (or lack of greeting), and a variety of other factors. All of these things set the initial tone for a relationship, and thus as leaders we need to pay attention to these factors. At the Big Oak Ranch--a Christian ministry for children, and the organization associated with the high school where I teach--one of the first things they teach children is how to give a firm handshake while looking someone in the eye. This is because many of the children there have not been taught how to do this, and their initial interactions with others are often either timid and nervous or aggressive and stand-offish. This simple skill helps the newly arrived children to begin setting a new tone in each new relationship they form. (If you'd like to learn more, please visit https://www.bigoak.org/ to get more information on this amazing organization).

Thus, in our leadership, we need to remember the phrase "Be the first...". As Christ first loved us and gave Himself up for us, so we must be willing to give ourselves for others even before they do so for us. This phrase also implies give and take, as we saw earlier: give respect and take responsibility. Give respect to each person you meet and take responsibility for the way in which you present yourself to them. Now, don't worry: this is not an entire chapter about image or presentation or personal branding or any of those things. But it is about how you present yourself to other people: be the first to give respect and to take responsibility.

Second, "be the first" means to be willing to reach out to someone who needs help, even if this is controversial or uncomfortable. Be the first to volunteer your services when they can meet a need for someone. Be the first to try to mend a broken or strained relationship. At the time of this writing, it is around Christmas 2017, and this is a difficult time of year for many people who have lost loved ones or other difficult emotional situations. So be the first to reach out and try to help: a parent to a child, a sister to a brother, or a friend to a friend.

Third, be the first to *forgive* others. As Christians we know that we have been forgiven much, and we also should remember that we are commanded to forgive others. It has been said (and attributed to various people) that "Holding on to anger is like drinking poison and expecting the other person to die." Regardless of who originally said this, there is much truth in it. We must be willing to let go of past hurts or offenses if we are to move forward from them. The scope of this book does not extend to trying to explain all of the difficulties (or solutions) to this; but it is imperative to our leadership that we learn to forgive.

As leaders we must also be the first to admit fault when we are wrong and be the first to share credit with other people when things go well. Very few leaders ever accomplish anything of value all on their own. There is almost always a team or group involved, so let's be sure to acknowledge that; it will go a long way in terms of relationship building and in the impact you will have on your audience. It is also evidence of humility to be able to encourage and applaud others' contributions instead of having to publicize one's own accomplishments.

Last, and most importantly, be the first to serve. As Christ washed the disciples' feet, as He gave Himself up for us, so we must be willing to serve others if we are to properly fulfill our roles as leaders. Always be willing to do the little bit extra, show up early, stay a bit late, go out of your way for others. All of these things essentially hit on the same idea. A key component of leadership is putting the needs of others before our own, in order to help them become better versions of themselves.

Part II: Be The First Is "The Golden Rule" Applied To Relationships.

When my dad was drafted to go fight in the Vietnam War, he was fortunate compared to many others that were drafted in that he had a college degree and was thus able to go to Officer Candidate School before heading to the war zone. When he got to Vietnam, he found a situation that was less than ideal: an entrenched opponent, no clear objective, many combat restrictions, and the difficulty of fighting an increasingly unpopular war with many soldiers who also had not chosen to be there. So what he did was the best he could, and by all accounts I've come across, both from soldiers' testimony and from various publications, he did his job well. After Dad died, I interviewed multiple men who served under his command in Vietnam, and as I did this, a common theme began to develop in the men's responses: not a single one of them initially liked Dad when they first met him. He was tough on them, he placed high expectations on them, and he demanded that they complete their jobs with excellence regardless of how they personally felt about each task. However, the longer they served under Dad the more they realized that these things were for their own good, and in time they even came to appreciate these aspects of Dad's leadership style.

A few years before his death in 2008 and thus decades after the end of the Vietnam War, Dad's company had a reunion that he was able to attend. Due to Dad's declining health--the previous year he had been diagnosed with a rare form of cancer, which has been tied to exposure to Agent Orange while serving in Vietnam--my younger sister accompanied Dad and was able to witness this event.

Many of the former enlisted men, others who were drafted for Vietnam but had not been able to go through officer training, were surprised and encouraged that their commanding officer bothered to come back to such an event. Apparently, this was not usual.

What these soldiers said at this event confirmed the impression I had gotten from interviewing some of them: they did not like Dad, but they came to respect and even appreciate him and his high standards and expectations. These men knew and acknowledged that Dad was doing his job while also looking out for their best interests in terms of safety in the larger context of fighting a war. Dad once told me that his job was to follow orders from above while also making sure as many of his men as possible could return home. This, to me, is the Golden Rule as applied to relationships and leadership: lead others as you would have them lead you. Dad did that, just as Christ did that for us.

Yes, Dad required his soldiers to go out on patrols the way they were supposed to; yes, he required them to perform guard duty even when they did not think it was necessary. And these things served the men well when they were attacked by a much larger Viet Cong force. The training, the high standards, and the requirement that every man know his job well all helped Dad's company to repel the attack without losing a single soldier. This is because these soldiers knew that Dad wanted each and every one of them to be able to go home; they knew he cared about them, even when he was strict toward them. They knew he wanted them to be as safe as possible, and therefore they were willing to do the difficult and risky tasks even when they did not want to.

People are inspired by and are willing to work harder for leaders when they know that the leader values them and shows that they are important. This begins with the relationship between the leader and the audience. Again, take care of relationships, and the results will take care of themselves. One of the key components about taking care of relationships is forgiveness. C.S. Lewis tells us,

"Never, ever pin all of our hopes on any human being because they will let us down." This is a harsh truth, but we do need to recognize its veracity.

We must be willing to forgive others when they make mistakes. To be unwilling to forgive mistakes means that we are implicitly requiring perfection, and that is always going to disappoint us. Rather than perfection, let us pursue and expect excellence while taking care of relationships. Being willing and able to forgive is absolutely crucial if we are to take care of any long-term relationship, whether in a leadership capacity or in our personal lives.

Part III: Results Are Often Self-Focused. Relationships Are People-Focused.

I am divorced and remarried, and there are many lessons I have learned from that process that are shared throughout this book. One of these lessons is the absolute importance of forgiveness in relationships. In a marriage, that means that each spouse is choosing to serve the other, and when that is done well, it is a beautiful thing. I have seen this both from doing it poorly--as in my first marriage that ended in divorce--and from trying to do it better in my second marriage, which is almost four years old now. I have also seen it from my wife, my ex-wife, and from her husband, as we all four try to work together for the good of our daughters (and also now for the good of my ex-wife's young son, a child from her second marriage). This includes each of the adults being respectful to each other, which sets a great example for the children. It also sets an important tone within our family structure, and this is something I learned from my mom and dad after their divorce and which Jesus so beautifully shows to each of us every day.

When I was in middle school, my parents divorced, and despite their divorce they remained friends until my father's death. In fact, when Dad's cancer caused him to move from my hometown of Anniston, Alabama, to Chattanooga, Tennessee, in order to have better medical care, Mom actually moved there as well in order to help take care of him. At that point, they had been divorced for over a decade. This was an amazing example of selflessness on Mom's part, and she got some negative feedback about it from various people who asked her why she chose to move there. She responded by saying that just because they had divorced did not mean that she had stopped caring about and respecting Dad. Mom was a nurse for many years, and she used all of that experience and compassion in helping take care of Dad through the end of his life. My brother and sister-in-law as well as my younger sister all lived in Chattanooga and helped Mom with that task. To me, that is an amazing example of taking care of relationships rather than simply trying to win arguments or focusing on results. It is also a beautiful picture of forgiveness and reconciliation: Mom and Dad did not remarry, but they remained friends who cared about each other and who encouraged each other.

At the beginning of the chapter, we asked the question of whether anyone really wins an argument with a loved one, and I believe even that whole structure or framework of trying to "win" an argument should be changed. The late great Stephen Covey, author of *Seven Habits of Highly Effective People* (and other bestsellers) wrote a chapter in that book called "Seek First to Understand Then to be Understood." The emphasis here is on making sure that we are truly listening to and grasping what another person is saying, and this is completely different than trying to 'win' an argument. This ability to listen well is a crucial aspect of leadership as well. A leader must be able to listen to the concerns of her audience and to understand the issues being faced, so that she may address the causes of the problem, rather than just tackling the symptoms.

Next, leaders must also remember that the way in which we speak is often just as important as what we say. The tone we use, the actions, the non-verbal aspects of our communication all factor into the way in which our message will be received. Anyone who has worked with children will tell you that children are naturally good at saying one thing while meaning something entirely different.

What we communicate, the message we actually send, is not just determined by our words. Most of us learned this when we were children and had gotten in trouble for something, and our parents forced us to say we were sorry to our sibling. Then, after saying a very unmeaningful and often mumbled, "Sorry," we were told, "This time, say it and mean it," in a very stern tone. In order to do this well, our body posture, our tone of voice, and even whether we were looking the other person in the eye or not--all of these things had to change if we were to 'mean it' when we apologized.

Think of a time when you were speaking to someone and you knew that the other person was truly invested in listening to you: looking you in the eye, paying attention, following your body language as well as the words you were speaking. When we do those things, we communicate that we respect and care about the person we are listening to. (For more info on this topic, I would recommend the book *Attention Pays* by Neen James.) Listening well and showing the other person that we value them by how we listen is a major component of what it means to "be the first."

Finally, we need to be the first to share credit with others when things go well. As a soccer coach, one of my favorite things to see is when a player scores a goal, instead of running off to celebrate on their own, the goal-scorer will look to find the player who passed them the ball or set up the scoring opportunity. I love to see players share credit by celebrating with their teammates, recognizing that no one person is solely responsible for the success of the team. I especially appreciate when the goal-scorers will look for and celebrate with the defenders who often get much less press and praise for their efforts, simply because their efforts are harder to measure and are thus less noticed. It's a bit like the difference between getting a promotion at work (recognition, pay increase, praise) and being a stay-at-home parent (no pay boost, little recognition, definitely not as much praise as you deserve, but still vitally important!).

The same principle holds true in leadership: rarely, if ever, do leaders accomplish anything of value alone. In fact, it never happens: leadership, by definition, means that there is a group or team being led, and therefore the success of the group is a result of the efforts of more than just the leader. We as leaders need to be humble enough to recognize and acknowledge that. Thus we need to be sure to celebrate the effort and contribution of every member of our teams.

Take a moment and remember the first time in your life when a respected adult in your world stopped and went out of their way to make a difference in yours. For me, one of these moments occurred in middle school, when I was in eighth grade and playing varsity soccer with the high school players. I was not one of the better players on the team, and I was smaller and younger than everyone else. At the end-of-season party the coach stopped me and said, "You know, Joel, you really should consider pursuing soccer as a type of career." At the time, I thought that meant that the coach felt I had the potential to become a professional soccer player. Whether that's what Coach McIntosh meant or not, I came to learn that I was not good enough to ever go pro. However, what his comment did inspire me to do was to consider making the game of soccer part of my career. As a result of that, I played in college (both in the United States and for one semester in the UK), and then after my playing career ended, I immediately began coaching and have been doing that ever since. Coaching soccer has had a huge influence on every area of my adult life, just as playing soccer had a huge influence on my youth and adolescence. Much of my adult life, then, has been influenced by one comment made by a soccer coach over twenty years ago.

Remember those times in your own life, and then stop and ask these questions: Who am I potentially influencing today? Who am I showing respect to? Who can I reach out to and help? What relationship can I go and mend? Who do I need to forgive in order to move forward and become a better leader? Be the first to reach out and to do those things.

"Reach out and help others. Be a vessel, be the change, be the difference, or be the inspiration. Shine your light as an example. The world needs more of that." - Germany Kent

Questions to Consider:

1. **How have you seen "Be the first" displayed well by leaders in your experience?**

2. **When have you seen relationships damaged because neither side was willing to reach out to the other?**

3. **Why do you think it is important for leaders to be the first to reach out to others in terms of reconciling relationships?**

Action Step:

Spend a few minutes considering people in your circle that you need to reach out to in order to reconcile, and then reach out to at least one of them.

Chapter 5

Stealing a Seat or Tripping a Traveler: Intentions vs. Outcomes...

In studying the Bible closely, we see that both our actions as well as our motives or intentions are of utmost importance. With Jesus, it was not just about giving Himself up for us; it was about doing it because it was God's will. We see this in how He prays aloud on multiple occasions, even stating that the reason for the prayer is so that others might know better what Jesus was doing. And as with all of the leadership principles in this book, there is an element of 'both-and' at play: in this chapter, we want to look at how focusing on intentions or outcomes changes our leadership and how we relate to others.

Part I: Is It The Thought That Counts, Or Is The Road To Hell Paved With Good Intentions?

In the Middle Ages, the most powerful institution in Europe was the Roman Catholic Church. The church was the largest landowner, the local priests were involved in the people's lives from birth until death, the church was responsible for helping the poor and caring for the sick, and the church also was seen as having power over the most important aspect of a person: his or her eternal soul. Thus, in the centuries before the Protestant Reformation, the Roman Catholic Church believed that part of its job was to make sure that church doctrine was taught accurately and without any dissent or disagreement to the people of Europe and beyond.

Despite much of the good that the church did--and there was a lot of good that the Medieval church did--this desire to stamp out any heresy (any beliefs or statements that went against official church teachings) led to many abuses, most notably by the Spanish Inquisition. The Inquisition was a type of church court established in the 15th century by Ferdinand of Aragon and Isabella of Castile, the same ruling couple that sponsored Columbus's first voyage in 1492. The purpose of the Inquisition was to stamp out heresy, and in order to do that, the leaders often resorted to torture in order to get people to confess to various heretical acts and statements.

Estimates about how many people were killed by the Inquisition vary widely, but at a minimum the number is in the thousands. Now, I believe that a commitment to teaching true doctrine is a good thing, just as teaching accurate history is a good thing. However, I also believe that the Inquisition may be the world's greatest example of something that was begun with a good motive but which also led to highly negative unintended consequences. The motives and the intentions were good, but judging through the lens of history, the results were negative.

In a somewhat different context, C.S. Lewis talks about how our motives and our intentions matter as much or even more than our actions and the outcomes that result from them. In *Mere Christianity,* Lewis talks about how if we were traveling on a train and we stepped away from our seat for a moment, if another person took our seat innocently unaware that the seat was claimed already, we are unlikely to be angry at the other traveler except for possibly a moment's annoyance. When our good sense kicks in, we realize they probably were unaware that we had been sitting there, and thus though we are inconvenienced, we are not really angry about it. It is a simple case of a misunderstanding.

This is then contrasted with someone who, while walking down a hallway, purposely though unsuccessfully puts out a leg to trip us. In this situation, even though the person trying to trip us was unsuccessful, we are going to be rightfully angry or irritated at them for their intent to harm us, even when we did not suffer any real consequences. I have always found this to be a very telling illustration since, in one situation we suffered a very real negative consequence, while in the other situation nothing bad actually happened to us. However, we are angry in the second case and not in the first. This is because of the intention of the person in the second situation contrasted with the innocent mistake of the first.

We see this everyday in a variety of contexts, especially when we are in leadership roles. That is, we see some people make innocent mistakes that we often are not angry about even if they have large consequences. We also see people who, through conscious neglect or lack of care, cause situations that could have become catastrophes. Even if the catastrophe is averted, the leader is often much more frustrated with the person who made a conscious bad decision than with the person whose mistake was much more innocent. Thus, this chapter will be showing how intentions matter but good intentions alone are not enough and also about how outcomes matter but not more than people and relationships. Therefore, as a leader, it is our job to find the balance between those things and, as in all cases, to err on the side of serving others and preserving relationships as much as possible.

Part II: Intentions Matter, But They Aren't Enough.

Most people are familiar with the expression, "It's the thought that counts," or, most often when talking with young children or athletes, "It's okay because you really tried." There is much truth in these statements. There are plenty of times in our lives when, even if the outcome is not what we would have chosen, the important thing is that we did our best, gave everything we had, and therefore we have nothing to regret. We teach this to children in athletics, and we see this all the time, especially when we see how our intentions reflect our values and our priorities. There is also truth here in relation to the grace of the Gospel: God expects perfection knowing we can't be perfect, and thus He sent Jesus to be perfection for us. This is both humbling and encouraging. But while we are on this side of eternity, our leadership must also take these things into account, knowing that while our intentions matter, good intentions alone are not good enough.

In 2016, the high school soccer team that I coach made it to the state championship game for the first time in our program's history. This important game was also magnified to me because it was the first time any team I had coached had ever made it beyond a state tournament semifinal game. My wife has always been very supportive of my coaching, and she regularly attended our games, especially in the playoffs. In fact, she had been at the game a week earlier when we defeated a team 2-0 that had beaten us 5-2 the previous year. However, on the day of the state championship game, my wife was unable to come and watch because she was out of town with a friend, on a trip they scheduled long before we realistically even considered being in the state championship match. She was at the direct opposite end of the state from where the game was taking place: the game was in Huntsville in north Alabama, and she was with a friend and her family in Mobile, on the Alabama coastline about 350 miles to the south. Unbeknownst to me, she and her friend left Mobile early enough that day so that my wife could try to make the long drive from Mobile, drop her friend in Birmingham (a little over halfway) and then still make it up to Huntsville in time to see the championship game and surprise me there.

Despite travel delays outside of her control and an overheating car engine which forced her to stop numerous times to put water in the radiator, my wife arrived at the tournament site in Huntsville...about ten minutes after the game ended with my team falling 4-1. Maryellyn actually called me from the parking lot right after the trophy presentation to let me know she had arrived, and she was very disappointed that she had not made it in time to see the game. Though I understood her disappointment--we both would have loved for her to have made it in time to see some of the game, obviously--I also reassured her that it was ok. I told her that this is absolutely an example of a situation in which the intention, the thought and goal behind her actions, mattered much more than the outcome.

Think about it: she left a vacation a day early, drove hundreds of miles in a car that began to not cooperate, and she did it all just to try to be there for me because she knew that it was an important event in my life. That intention and willingness to sacrifice herself reflected her priorities and values: she wanted me to know that she loves me, and she wanted do that by being there with me on what remains one of the most important days of my professional career. And though she did not arrive as early as she had hoped, she was able to make it and show me that she wanted to support me, even when it came at a great cost of time and effort to herself.

When I reflect on that match, a few specific things immediately spring to mind. First, I'm reminded by how surreal it felt to actually be in a state championship game as a coach. Second, I remember all of my players being completely exhausted, with one of my senior captains coming off the field after the game with multiple coin-sized blisters on the bottom of her foot that had split open from her effort of running so much. Third, and by far the most important, I remember my wife's effort to get to Huntsville just to support me in my coaching. When I think about that day, I am also reminded of a lyric from one of my favorite bands, Matchbox20. In one of their songs from my adolescence they sang something that is amazingly applicable here: "You can still lose even if you really try." All of us really tried that day, with the best of intentions, and all of us still lost.

Another great historical example of losing even when you really try is seen from the World War I invasion of Gallipoli, planned by none other than the future Prime Minister of Great Britain, Winston Churchill. A large force of Allied soldiers made up of mainly French and British troops invaded this Dardanelles area with the aim of capturing Constantinople (present-day Istanbul), the capital of the Ottoman Empire (mostly present-day Turkey). After eight months of fighting, the Allies were defeated in what would prove to be the only major Ottoman victory of the entire war, and the Allied troops were then withdrawn to go and fight elsewhere. In the grand scheme of the war, the defeat was a disaster for the Allies even though they went on to win World War I. Again, the point of the invasion was to capture the Ottoman capital and knock the Turks out of the war. This failed spectacularly, despite the best efforts and intentions of the Allies, and it is viewed somewhat more positively these days since the lessons learned from that campaign helped the World War II Allies be more informed and effective at planning the Normandy Invasion (D-Day) of 1944. However, at the time, and for many years afterward, Gallipoli stood as an example of great intentions that failed to produce a desired outcome.

Here we see the somewhat difficult truth or paradox: no matter how good the intention may be, if the execution is poor, the result will be negative. At the same time, even if the result is not what would have been preferred, it is hard to find too much fault with a situation in which all of the intentions were meant well. As leaders, we need to learn this. The intentions absolutely matter: *why* we do things is often just as important as *what* we do, especially in the context of the Gospel. If we are doing great things, but we are doing them for ultimately self-serving ends rather than for the sake of Christ, these great things will become meaningless in the end. The intentions matter, but intentions alone are not enough.

In the case of Maryellyn coming to watch the soccer game in Huntsville, the intention was amazingly there, but she was still upset about not quite making it in time to see the game. In terms of the invasion of Gallipoli, the intentions again were great, but the outcome did not result in the desired aims for that campaign. Another saying that many people are familiar with is that, "The road to hell is paved with good intentions." There are many things that we think about, intend to do, or mean to do but that we never actually get around to accomplishing. In leadership, this is not good enough: we must follow-through with our good intentions, and we must pay attention to the outcomes.

It sounds very high-minded to only focus on the intentions, but the truth is that history is littered with well-intended ideas that proved to be disastrous failures. Communism always comes to my mind as the greatest example of this: everyone contributes, everyone shares equally, and everyone lives happily ever after...except that in reality a few people control everything, everyone else barely survives, governments become dictatorships, and the entire system eventually destroys itself the way Communism predicted capitalism would do. As Christian leaders, we should be especially wary of any system that is based on an assumption of human goodness. No matter how well-intended or well-structured such a system may be, it is doomed to fail due to man's inherent sinfulness and corruption.

As an educator, another example of this is the No Child Left Behind Act, along with many other laws that focus on trying to get students to pass certain grade levels or to at least perform better in the classroom and on standardized tests. These laws are almost always well-intended, but the reality is that most of the time it causes a negative effect: students often pass who should not, because the school system and/or the individual teachers, rather than the students, get in trouble if too many students fail. The intent of such laws is always to help students perform better; the outcome is that often students perform even more poorly because they know that the schools are the ones who will suffer if the students do not perform well. As a result of that, the outcomes are not what were intended. Again, intentions matter, but they alone are not enough.

Part III: Outcomes Matter, But Not More Than People And Relationships.

In my first year as a high school head coach, I was at a small Christian school in Fayetteville, North Carolina. Midway through the season, we were playing a game against a rival Christian school from across town. That season our rivals had a good team led by a phenomenal young player who was the focus of their attack. The first time we played them we tied them, and so the second time we faced them I decided that we were not going to let this young player keep them in the game. In order to accomplish this, I told my captain, a senior and a very skilled and hard-working player named *Brent that every time their star touched the ball, I wanted Brent to knock him down. Sure, go for the ball, get it as much as you can, but make sure that no matter what he hits the ground every single time he touched the soccer ball.

Brent, despite some misgivings, faithfully carried out my instructions during the game, and their star must have hit the ground hard at least a dozen times. With about five minutes left, and while we were holding on to a slim lead, Brent was finally thrown out of the game for what is called 'persistent infringement,' which is soccer talk for "continuing to do something that is against the rules over and over and over." Brent came off the field, and I thanked him for doing exactly as I had instructed him, and we ended up winning the game and defeating our rivals for the first time in a couple of years.

The question is: was that worth it? At that point in my career, I was a young coach who was selfishly focused on building a reputation as a winner, and thought that I could do so by being successful in big games such as that one. Thus at the time, I really believed the answer was yes. At this point, I realize that I could not have been more wrong. The answer, emphatically, is NO, it was not worth what I did to win that game. What I did was to set a terrible example based on poor values and selfish ends, and what it led to was a damaged relationship with a player and his family due to my actions. By setting that example, what I was showing everyone with eyes to see was that I valued winning over principles, and that I valued short-term success over long-term relationship building and value-teaching. I showed that I was more interested in victory on the field than about teaching life lessons that would carry on far beyond Brent's soccer career. Brent, if you ever read this, please know that I am sorry and hope you can forgive me for that poor example.

Outcomes do matter, especially as leaders. We have goals, or quotas, or something, and these things have to be accomplished. But outcomes do not matter more than relationships, not if we are focused on eternity. Outcomes are important because they show a level of commitment and effort devoted to accomplishing a task. There are certain leadership roles in which you will be judged almost solely on the outcomes: CEOs, professional (and often high school and college) sports coaches, direct sales positions, etc. In many positions, the only criteria used for judging your performance is outcomes. Outcomes most certainly matter. For the Christian leader, though, we must remember that even our earthly outcomes must be subject to the greater eternal outcome of our actions, decisions, and intentions.

Even though some roles will be based solely on outcomes, in most leadership roles we will be judged by a combination of factors including both our intentions and our outcomes. The outcomes may hold more weight simply because they are more noticeable, more measurable, and more public. Another great example of this is Marv Levy, the head coach of the NFL's Buffalo

Bills football team during much of the 1990s. Even today, two decades later, he remains the only NFL coach to take a team to four straight Super Bowl appearances. Unfortunately for him, depending on how you look at it, his Bills lost all four of those Super Bowls, and so his name is often overlooked when casual fans have the water-cooler conversation of "greatest NFL coaches of all time." This is simply because he lost the four Super Bowls that his teams went to, and in his position, people judge based almost solely on results. Had his team won any one of those games, he would get much more respect (that he, in my opinion, very rightly deserves) as one of the game's greatest-ever coaches.

Fortunately for most of us, we will not be professional coaches, whose whole career is judged simply on the results of a few games. We will be judged on both our intentions and results, and at the end of the day, when you look back as a leader, you need to know the answer to this question: what are you going to want to see, results or relationships, intentions or outcomes? Are you going to want to know that you made an impact on people, that you were able to help others become better versions of themselves (even if you did not win as many games as you would have liked), or are you going to point to awards, trophies, accolades, and recognitions? Are you going to point to individual accomplishments, or are you going to point to the ways in which you were able to help people become better people? Are you going to point to your earthly success, or to your eternal outcomes?

Part IV: Find The Balance.

As we have seen, intentions matter but they alone are not enough. There are plenty of well-intended mistakes in the world. As we have also seen, outcomes matter but not more than people. Outcomes should not be focused on at the expense of relationships. So what does all of this mean for us as leaders? It means that you have to decide what to focus on at different times and stages of your career, seeking to balance between good intentions and positive outcomes all while keeping in mind the ultimate aim of furthering the Gospel. You need to see what is most appropriate based on your particular leadership journey and based on where your group is in its particular lifetime or shelf-life (i.e., a group you have for a weekend project vs. a program you are building that may last decades).

It means that you need to find the balance between focusing on relationships and results, between intentions and outcomes. As we have also seen, if you take care of relationships the results will take care of themselves. If you start with good intentions, then the outcomes will more often than not also be positive. At the time of this writing, I am about to start my fifth season coaching soccer at the same high school, and in that time we have improved greatly, including making state championship game appearances in each of the past two seasons.

Unfortunately, we lost both of those games. After the first one, I was unable to go to sleep that night because I was so focused on thoughts of what we might have done differently to get a different outcome from that game and what we could do better the following year. This past year, after making the championship game again, we lost to a different team by a similar scoreline. In the year between those two games, I spent much time thinking about what it meant to make it to that level and what we should do to try to sustain that level of success in the future. In that time I also realized a very important truth which I then began telling my players and students at every opportunity: twenty years from now, even just five years from now, almost no one in that high school will remember those trips to the state championship game. The kids who were on the team will graduate and move on, new players will take their place, and the memory will fade. The trophies will get dusty, the trophy case will get walked past with fewer and fewer glances at what is inside, and the pictures in the hallway will get moved and make way for more recent ones of other successful teams in other sports.

Five years from now, what will matter much more than any trophy we could win are the relationships those players built and the lessons they learned through being a part of our soccer program. What will matter are our relationships with each other and the Lord, and the way in which the players apply the lessons learned from soccer in other areas of their lives. They will go on to college or the workforce. They will get married and become wives and mothers as well as teachers and doctors and artists and engineers. And when they do those things, the trophies we did or did not win will matter less and less. Could we have done things differently to maybe win one or both of those games? Perhaps. But we did the best we could, and that is all I can ask for from my players. Remember, "You can still lose even if you really try." This does not mean that we give up and say that outcomes do not matter; they do. But it also means that we do not only focus on intentions, because no one who has a competitive bone in her body can play without wanting to win.

As a leader, our job is to find the balance between outcomes and intentions. And when we are in doubt as to what decision to make or path to follow, we must always try to err on the side of serving others, preserving relationships with our audience, and serving the Kingdom. For me, this means that no matter how many games we win, my first priority is to help these young players learn lessons that will help them become better people, so that when their playing days are finished they are better equipped for the rest of their lives. My intention is to help them become better versions of themselves, and the outcome of those intentions will only truly be seen in their lives beyond high school.

"What matters is your intentions and your behavior." - C.S. Lewis

Questions to Consider:

1. How important are a person's or group's intentions in terms of shaping a leader's response in a given situation?

2. How important are outcomes in your specific leadership roles?

3. When have you been guilty of sacrificing a relationship in order to achieve something, and how can you make sure to avoid that in the future?

Action Step:

Take a few minutes to write down a few ways that you can better take care of relationships within your leadership roles.

Chapter 6

Selling History to High-School Students:

"Lead Through Learning"--What does that look like?

As Christian leaders, we must constantly be seeking out deeper and fuller knowledge of God through studying His Word. We should also be focused on learning how to become better leaders in the various roles we will fulfill throughout our lifetimes. Sometimes this is done formally, as in a college or high school, and sometimes this is done informally, as in a small group or through independent reading. But however it is pursued, we must constantly be seeking out more and more knowledge. As C.S. Lewis said in *Mere Christianity*, "God is no fonder of intellectual slackers than of any other slackers. If you are thinking of becoming a Christian, I warn you, you are embarking on something which is going to take the whole of you, brains and all." As Christian leaders, we must engage our hearts and our minds as we pursue Godly leadership in our lives.

Part I: Why Education Matters.

I love the television show 'Scrubs' even though I've only seen the first couple of seasons. In one of the episodes guest star

Dick Van Dyke plays the character of an older doctor in the hospital. In the show, he takes the main character (Dr. Dorian, or "JD") under his wing for a couple of different procedures. During one scene, Dick Van Dyke's character performs a procedure that is somewhat outdated and is not commonly used anymore, despite JD's misgivings. The audience learns that this procedure is not commonly used anymore because it has higher risks associated with it than more recently-developed techniques.

As a result of this procedure, the patient has a negative reaction, and JD feels compelled to report this to the hospital even though the Chief of Medicine at the hospital, Dr. Kelso, is good friends with Dick Van Dyke's character. Because of JD's report, the hospital launches an inquiry into the situation, and Dick Van Dyke's character ends up losing his job. Dr. Kelso is very upset with JD for bringing this to his attention even though he knows JD did the right thing. In a moving scene toward the end of the episode, Dr. Kelso ends up having to explain to his friend that the reason he lost his job is simply because he fell behind; that is, he did not do what was necessary to stay up to date, and as a result, the hospital could no longer employ him.

This story illustrates an important aspect of leadership, and that is that leaders must continually be staying up to date and informed about new techniques, procedures, and philosophies in our particular areas of involvement, while also remaining true to our foundational principles and beliefs. For me, that means paying attention to how education and soccer coaching are changing and evolving both in the classroom and outside of it. Your areas of involvement may be drastically different, but the key component is the same: ***leaders must be learners***, and we must always be looking for ways to continue educating ourselves and learning more about our chosen fields. Education is extremely important even though that may not mean a formal, classroom-style education.

The second reason this is important is that Golden Rule revisited: lead how you want to be led. Most of us want to be led by someone who is constantly learning and growing rather than being led by someone who simply refuses to learn due to pride or laziness. Remember the great quote from Coach John Wooden: "When you're through learning, you're through." So let's explore this idea of leaders as learners.

Part II: Leaders ARE Learners, And So Is Everyone Else.

The old adage that "You learn something new every day," is entirely true. The question is what are you learning, and where are you learning that information? In other words, where is your newly-acquired knowledge coming from? In our increasingly digital age, the answer to the first question is becoming more and more vague because the answer to the second question is more diverse than it has ever been. That is, because we are learning from so many different sources, the information we are learning is less systematized than it has ever been. As Christian leaders and learners, we have a duty to look into not just what we are learning, but also the source of that new information. We also have a duty to evaluate new information in light of the Bible to see how it lines up. We pick up snippets of things from social media or news headlines, and so what we are learning is much more scattered. The effects of this are both positive and negative.

On the positive side, we have access to more information, from a wider variety of sources than humans have ever had before. On the negative side, because the information we are getting is less systematized and organized, it means that there is a good chance that we are missing out on important information that we otherwise would have gotten. Therefore, as leaders, we must constantly be asking ourselves "What am I learning?" and "Where am I getting my information?" and then evaluating our answers to see where we may have gaps in our knowledge.

I speak to my students very often about my view of education so that I can communicate that to them, especially when they lose sight of the larger purpose of education. And let's be honest: how many of us had a great 'big picture' view of education when we were freshmen in high school? I know I didn't, and I think it's safe to assume that many students today are in a similar situation. Because of this, a couple years ago I was able to address the student body in one of our chapel services, and I shared a speech called, "What Are You Doing Here?" The point of this was to ask the students that question and to get them to ask themselves that question, because their answers are very telling. The different answers the students gave showed them some of their own views about education: get good grades, prepare for a job, etc.

I also helped students think about education differently simply by emphasizing each word in the question differently: "WHAT are you doing here?" is a very different question than "What are you DOING here?" And so the different way of asking the question also helped garner different responses. When we then explored these different responses, we were able to discuss different views of education that I then tried to pass on to the students: education is about learning different skill sets--such as reading, writing, and thinking--and it is about learning values--such as humility, empathy, and compassion.

When we talk about leaders as learners, we need to have a clear focus of what our leadership role is. This allows us to then figure out how to improve our leadership through learning new techniques, utilizing different tools, and expanding our knowledge in applicable areas. There are many different ways to do this, more today than ever before: books, web-based classes, CEUs, role models, heroes, mentors, coaches. There is an almost limitless supply of great learning resources, and as leaders it is our task to be seeking those out. If you go back and look through the book, you'll see a number of these mentioned in various chapters throughout. So we've seen that leaders are learners. Now the question is, how do we make sure that we are continuing to learn as we grow in our leadership roles?

Part III: Learning As An Act Of Humility.

To admit that we still have things to learn takes a certain amount of humility. That is, to learn is to admit that we don't already know all that we need to, and it is to admit that we do not already have all of the answers or information that we require. It takes a certain amount of humility to willingly confess this, and when we do, that is when we begin to consciously grow. Refusing to learn something, on the other hand, is typically either an act of pride ("I don't need to know this") or laziness ("I don't feel like learning this"). Most of the time these statements are made by people who are convinced that they do not need to learn new information, and this misplaced self-assurance is, again, typically the result of pride.

Upon taking up a recently-created post at the University of Cambridge, the beloved author and professor C.S. Lewis once referred to himself as a "dinosaur," a holdover from an earlier intellectual age that has long since gone out of fashion. He was a medievalist, trying to teach and influence an increasingly modern (and now postmodern) world. I am no C.S. Lewis, so I will resist referring to myself as a dinosaur; I also am not writing here about intellectual or educational philosophy, but about leadership. As such, I am not so much a dinosaur as I am a Luddite in a tech world.

A Luddite is defined as someone who actively opposes more industrialization or new technology, and if you were to ask any of my students--especially in today's smartphone generation--they could tell you stories of the many times I have quite willingly hopped on my intellectual soapbox about the dangers of smartphones, their negative effects on learning, and the overall deteriorating effect on classroom learning due to electronic devices. However that may be, I also am forced to acknowledge that I personally and we as a society have tremendously benefited from technology, and therefore to oppose it on principle would be an act not of mere selfishness but of true pride.

Pride has been defined in many ways, and I want to begin by saying that not all 'pride' is a bad thing. Again, referencing C.S. Lewis, he wrote (my paraphrase here) that pride in one's regiment or in one's family, or in anything else that focuses outward, is not a bad thing, especially if that causes a person to work harder or serve others in pursuit of improving the regiment, family, etc. No, the dangerous type of pride is what we often think of as competitiveness, that is, pride that is constantly weighing ourselves against others. This pride is dangerous specifically because it is so self-centered, self-focused, and self-serving.

So, back to me being a Luddite: I willingly admit that I am often opposed to new technology simply because it is new and I don't understand it. However, because of my pride, I am also opposed to it because I don't want to be bothered with having to learn it, and because it is so much easier for people younger than me to grasp. This is brought home to me every time a student references a new app, or social media platform, or even popular video game about which I have no idea.

When I was a kid, the most popular gaming platform was the original Nintendo, the 8-bit NES with Mario Brothers and Duck Hunt. I was never great at it, but I got pretty good. And then the Super Nintendo came out, and the controllers had more buttons, and, try though I might, I never could get good with that many buttons. As a result, I was strongly opposed to the system, and I have been opposed to every system that has come out since. In college, when my dorm mates were playing on N64s or GameCubes or other systems, I would mostly watch, or I would play and get destroyed, and both of those things wounded my pride.

After college, when texting was first growing in popularity, I refused to even try to learn how to do it, just on principle. As smartphones have become more popular, I did the same thing, refusing to buy a smartphone until less than two years ago when my old phone finally died. Sure, I endured much ribbing about my Luddite-tendencies, but I believed I had the moral high ground...until I realized that the only reason I was opposed to all of those things was pride and laziness. I didn't want to admit that I would need help learning new technology, because that would make me seem less intelligent than I like to think I am. I didn't want to admit that, though there are dangers, perhaps the technology itself isn't the problem--though I will always believe that the technology enables people to make bad decisions more easily, as I have seen in my own life and in the lives of others. I certainly didn't want to give up my pride-based moral high ground regarding technology. I was too comfortable in my pride.

And then, through the grace of God, He reminded me of humility, of the many times I have had to ask for help because I could not, on my own, do what needed to be done. Without help from others, I could not fulfill my responsibilities. I remembered that, even without smartphone technology, I had made more mistakes (with bigger consequences) than I had thought myself capable of. It was in that moment of God-revealed clarity that I realized learning is an act of humility. The reason this is so important is because, if we are not willing to admit that we don't already know everything, we run the risk of believing that we know much more than we do. And believing we know more than we do is one of the biggest mistakes that a leader can make. Allow me to illustrate.

In late February of 2017, I was involved in a significant car wreck while traveling home from soccer practice. It was dark, it was raining, and while I was driving at 65 mph down Highway 431 in Alabama a large truck pulled out from a gas station when I was about fifty yards away. For some reason, the truck was slow to pull across my two lanes, and so as I approached, I was faced with having to make one of three choices: 1) pull my car right, off the road, and into a ditch; 2) go straight into the side of the truck (I drive a small sedan) at high speed; 3) pull my car left into oncoming traffic. Now, when I tell this story to my high school students, the typical question I get is, "Why didn't you just hit the brakes?" usually asked in a tone of condescension reserved only for those who are blissfully ignorant of key aspects of a discussion.

In response, depending on my level of patience that day, I explain a few things to my students, most of whom are either freshmen or sophomores whose average driving experience is less than a year: 1) that hitting the brakes on a wet road at 65 mph wouldn't have actually stopped the car in the space available; and 2) it might cause hydroplaning, causing me to have even less control of the car; and 3) it's always interesting that people who don't really know how to drive or have much experience driving feel qualified to give advice to people who do, without really thinking about it.

To be fair to my students, all generations have the tendency to assume they know better than previous generations, and so my students may or may not be any more arrogant than we were as children. In fact, I would argue that the propensity to assume we know much more than we do is something of which we are all guilty, especially in today's society with its 24/7 Internet access.

That is, as leaders and simply as people, we often have a tendency to assume that we know much more than we actually do. Students are convinced they don't need to study because they can simply look up whatever they need to know using Wikipedia or similar sites; parents are convinced that they know as much as doctors because they spent time researching on WebMD; and people like myself are convinced that we're smarter than everyone else simply because we try to remain informed about news, sports, current events, etc.

As if this illusion of enlightenment wasn't enough, the tendency to have our preconceptions or assumptions confirmed is often furthered by the self-imposed echo chambers of social media. On our Facebook, Twitter, and Instagram feeds, we are often only exposed to articles or statements that confirm our own opinions, confirming what we already know, or think we know. This often happens without our knowledge, thanks to the various algorithms used by social media programs, and so we believe we are seeing the whole story while someone with opposite opinions is just ignoring the facts. This in turn reinforces our belief that we know what we think we know, and it also lessens the likelihood that we'll continue our research with openness, since we're already convinced that we're right. And as leaders, this is extremely dangerous territory.

If we are to lead well, we must 1) be aware of the dangers of this situation, and 2) take steps to avoid it and to lessen the effects of it when we have already fallen prey. In leadership positions, we are often the decision makers, the managers, the ones responsible for making things function the way they are supposed to. As a result of that, we are in danger of, as coaches are often warned about, "believing our own press," or becoming satisfied in our own knowledge and expertise. When that occurs, our leadership is likely to stagnate, since we are no longer pursuing ways to improve because we are already convinced that we know what we're doing. We may not think of it in these terms, but this pattern can be observed in many situations: husbands who become inattentive of their wives, coaches who lose the commitment of their players, teachers who refuse to consider new methods or different classroom projects, etc. In all of these situations, the result is the same: the illusion of enlightenment leads to a lack of continued intellectual growth.

Thus, after becoming aware of these dangers and the negative results that inevitably follow, we must examine our current leadership situations and see where we have already become stagnant, and we must takes steps to correct this. In short, we must begin anew the process of becoming a leader, an expert, a student.

The solution, then, is humility: we must be willing to admit that we don't know as much as we think we do, and we must back this up by seeking information even when we think we are already experts in our given areas. We must purposefully seek out new information, even from sources we know we disagree with. We must humbly ask others for guidance or suggestions, and we must be willing to consider their answers, rather than immediately rejecting them based on our previously held assumptions.

The purpose of leadership is to positively influence others in whatever roles we are in. This can be accomplished in a wide variety of ways, in different stages, at different times. But throughout all of those, the danger of becoming self-satisfied, of becoming prideful, of being convinced that we know best, is ever-present. The danger of pride in knowledge is very real, especially for those of us in professions that involve teaching and coaching, and thus our response must be conscious, it must be intentional, and it must be continual. Good leadership is crucial, and in our ever-changing world, good leadership requires constant learning, an open mind, and a willingness to entertain alternate viewpoints while remaining true to the teachings of Scripture.

Being a high school history teacher is to walk into a classroom every day knowing that at the beginning of each semester almost none of the students I have are interested in learning about the subject I love. So my first job is not just to teach them the history; my first job is to 'sell' them the idea that history is useful. I have to 'sell' history as a discipline to students, to convince them that all those bold print names and terms are still relevant and important in their tech-heavy, teenage worlds. The first thing I have to do is to convince them that what they will be studying and learning is information and skills sets that can and will change their lives.

As leaders, we must understand that this is our fundamental task in every role. There is always more to learn, and everything we do has the potential to change people's lives through the power of the Gospel. Or, as Mr. Miagi said in the classic movie *Karate Kid*, "Someone always knows more." This is true, whether we want to admit it or not, and so we must be willing to go out of our way to continually seek new knowledge. For leaders, this means our journey of learning never ends.

"Keen perception and Christ-like humility are compatible." - Dr. Bill Davis

Questions to Consider

1. **Why is education such an important part of being a leader?**

2. **Do you think that continually pursuing knowledge automatically makes a person a better leader? Why or why not?**

3. **Do you think that learning really is an act of humility? Why or why not?**

Action Step:

Take time to think about what knowledge you need to pursue today in order to be a better leader tomorrow, and write down two ways that you can begin that pursuit.

Chapter 7

What Are You Doing Here?
Education vs. Experience

In leadership, we often face a false dichotomy in terms of importance: that is, we are either told that education helps us learn or that experience is the best teacher. Looking to the example of Christ, I believe His life shows that both are necessary for proper instruction. Jesus both instructed the crowds and the apostles using stories and parables, and He also lived and traveled with the apostles for years, showing them how His teachings applied in various situations. If we are to be Godly leaders, we must understand that both education and experience are necessary parts of our growth.

Part I: My Older Brother Is Smarter Than Me.

My older brother, John, is one of the most intelligent people that I know, and he always has been. As a teenager, I was arrogant enough to think that he was one of the only people that was actually smarter than me! Oh, how I have learned since then. He is still smarter than me, but now I realize that he is by no means the only one.

Lead Others Better By Forgetting About Yourself

When John was in middle school, he was identified by the Duke TIP (Talent Identification Program) as a gifted student. In high school, he was invited to attend the Alabama School of Math and Science, a prestigious boarding school located in Mobile. He agreed to go there starting at the beginning of his junior year. By the middle of his senior year, he had dropped out and come home. Despite that, he applied to attend Jacksonville State University, and because of his high standardized test scores and after having gotten his GED certificate, John was awarded a scholarship to JSU. He then dropped out of JSU after a couple semesters. It was frustrating to the family to see John 'waste' his academic talent by dropping out rather than continuing his studies in the traditional way: high school, college, work. However, God had a different plan for John.

These days, he works at Blue Cross-Blue Shield of Tennessee at their Chattanooga campus, a giant glass-encased building overlooking the Tennessee River. Through the work he does and the projects he is involved in, John is making a huge difference in the lives of people all over the state and especially in Chattanooga. He has had a great time there for the last ten years, seeing steady increases in both salary and responsibility while continuing to work his way up in the company. He has gotten so good at what he does that for the past few years his company has flown him all over the US to give presentations on various topics and projects.

John is a great example of how intelligence, ability, and hard work can overcome not having a formal degree up to a certain level. However, in many industries there is often a ceiling that caps how far up you can go unless you are the entrepreneur, and John ran into that as well until he went back and finished his college education a couple of years ago. For leaders, this begs the question: which matters more, education or experience? I would argue that the answer is: neither matters more, and both are important.

Part II: Education Matters, But It Alone Isn't Enough.

For the purpose of this chapter, the word 'education' refers to formal education in a classroom or online setting. And when discussing the merits of formal education with students, I often hear the same counter-argument, and it typically revolves around the example of Bill Gates. Students refer to him and say something like, "Well, he dropped out of college, and he's still a huge success." And while that is true, I also like to remind students that, before he dropped out of college he was smart and/or hard-working enough to get into Harvard. I then ask if any of them plan on applying to Harvard with a realistic chance of getting in. If not, then the point tends to hit home pretty quickly that though he did not graduate college, he still had to work hard to educate himself in order to succeed.

As a teacher, I would be completely remiss if I said that education doesn't matter. I believe that education matters for many reasons. As I said in the previous chapter, I believe that the purpose of education is to teach students basic skills such as reading, writing, and critical thinking; education is also--and maybe more importantly-- about teaching students values, to teach them how to become better versions of themselves. For over a decade now, I have taught history and Bible classes and coached soccer, and so for me those are the mediums through which I try to help students become better people. There are many excellent Biblical and life lessons that can be seen in both classroom and academic settings, and I'm thankful that God has used me in this way. He also continues to humble me by reminding me that though I'm the teacher and coach, I also don't know it all.

In order to remind both myself and my students of our shared task of growing closer to God through academics and soccer, I continually focus on the phrase, "What are you doing here?" A couple of years ago, I wrote out my educational beliefs beginning with that question and following up with four different answers.

That list of answers to the question is posted on my classroom door, on the wall behind my podium, and on the wall above my white board: it is in front of students every day because I believe it is important to remind ourselves of what we are doing there. In my teaching and coaching, I try to focus on teaching specific values and skill sets, using history and soccer as the vehicle to drive that learning.

One thing that I focus on is teaching what have historically been referred to as the Four Cardinal Virtues: justice, temperance, prudence, and fortitude. These are values that have been taught to students throughout most of the history of western civilization, and they are values that are crucial to us becoming better people today. These virtues were briefly mentioned earlier in the book, and so now I want to explore them a bit more deeply.

Justice refers to what we would call the Golden Rule of "Treat others the way you want to be treated." It refers to dealing honestly and fairly with others. Temperance (despite how the word was misapplied in American history to refer solely to alcohol consumption) refers to doing things at the right time, to the right degree, and in the right way. It refers to moderation rather than going to extremes, whether the activity be eating and drinking or focusing our attention on sports. Prudence refers to using common sense, to thinking through the consequences of our actions before we do something. It has to do with using sound judgment. And Fortitude refers to what we would call courage, in multiple senses of the word. It certainly refers to overcoming fear, but it also refers to the type of courage it takes to do the right thing even when it is difficult. It refers to what we would call 'guts' or 'stick-to-it-ive-ness'. These virtues form the basis for the type of person that we should all strive to be, and thus these are the basis for the values of the Gospel that we seek to teach students: kindness, generosity, humility, grace, empathy, and many others.

Education is important for teaching the virtues, values, and skill sets mentioned above, and there are many different types and levels of education. Formal education often refers to high school and college, though there are also various types of certification programs and continuing education program out there. But there is also a difference between theoretical knowledge and practical knowledge. Most teachers will tell you that there is a huge gap between learning theory in a college class and then actually teaching a group of high-energy young people.

I have now been teaching for over a decade, but when I began I simply had a degree in history rather than education. I had done no student teaching, and I had only taken one education class; therefore, my first semester as a teacher in a classroom was very much a learning experience for me. I would not necessarily recommend this as the way to go, because the purpose of student-teaching is to help bridge the gap between the theory learned in class and the practical work of managing a classroom.

We also see the gap between theoretical knowledge and practical knowledge in other areas, such as kicking a soccer ball or welding metal or framing a house. These are skills that you can watch videos of, read books about, and talk with people about; but until you actually do those activities, your theoretical knowledge is very limited in terms of its usefulness. The best way to learn how to do any of these activities is to go and do them under the direction and supervision of someone who knows how to do them well.

Those of us with children have also seen this when it comes to teaching people how to drive. I teach high school freshmen and sophomores, and so many students are getting their permits or licenses during their semesters in my classroom, and even these students see that there is a massive difference between passing a multiple-choice test about driving and being able to parallel park a car.

For a leader, education matters, but the theoretical knowledge is not going to be enough, just as in our spiritual lives we should be studying the Word but also applying it in how we live.

Part III: Experience Matters, But It Is Limited In Scope

"Experience, that most brutal of teachers. But you learn; my God do you learn." This quote is often attributed to C.S. Lewis, and most of us would agree that experience is an amazing teacher in a lot of ways. Experience is extremely important to a leader, but it is kind of a catch-22. Remember filling out job applications as a younger person? You don't yet have much experience, so much of the application was blank. Then you go in for an interview only to find out that the company "only likes to hire people with experience." If you're like many people, you may remember being frustrated and thinking to yourself, "If you only hire people with experience already, how does anyone ever get started?!" This is a particularly frustrating situation, and so we then have to find creative ways to gather and gain experience before applying for those jobs again.

Experience is a key component of leadership, and it illustrates something that I want to really emphasize for leaders: *every role you are in is either a leadership role, or it is preparing you (giving you experience to help you) for a future leadership role.* Then your job becomes showing people how your experiences can help you. The major problem with experience, though, is that it is limited in scope: it is not possible for one person to experience everything.

I have heard many people in my life talk about how they do not really learn from other people's mistakes. They say that the only way they can learn something is through experiencing it for themselves. I understand that, and there is a sense in which that is true: until a person has experienced certain things, they do not fully realize the impact or effect that experience contains. If you have lost a loved one, you know what I am referring to; if you have not yet lost a loved one, be thankful and also realize that until you do, you will not fully understand what it is like. Having said that, there is also a sense in which the idea of "I have to experience it for myself to understand it" is a bit flawed because we all know that there are plenty of things that are not at all worth experiencing if it can be helped!

I do not have to experience it to know that it is painful to be shot or hit with a taser. That may sound extreme, but it is true, just as it is true that I will not fully comprehend the pain unless I am unfortunate enough to be shot or tased. But I do not have to go through it to know it hurts. The example serves to illustrate the point: experience can be a great teacher, but it is also limited in scope. On the other hand, some things are best learned through experience, such as raising children. There are hundreds or even thousands of books on child-rearing, child behavior, child psychology, child behavioral psychology, and other related topics. The truth is, until you have been around children and experienced the day-to-day difficulties of trying to teach them values and manners in the midst of everyday life, all of the book knowledge in the world is of limited value. So, we see that education and experience are both important for leaders.

The more positive experiences you can accumulate, the more first-hand knowledge you will have to guide you in future situations, especially if you can then combine your experiences with a willingness and ability to also learn from other people's experiences. One of the keys to remember here is humility: because we cannot learn everything via experience or formal education, we need to be actively seeking out ways to learn from those with more experience. We need to be humble enough to ask questions and learn so that we can, as far as possible, avoid making the same mistakes that others have already made.

Lead Others Better By Forgetting About Yourself

The school I teach at is associated with the Big Oak Boys Ranch and the Big Oak Girls Ranch, located in north-central Alabama. The Ranch is "A Christian home for children needing a chance." Many of the children who arrive at the Ranch come from very difficult backgrounds, and almost all of them have been either abused or abandoned before they arrive. The founder of the Ranch is a man named Mr. John Croyle (and his amazing wife Mrs. Tee). Mr. John, as I hear him most commonly referred to, was an All-American football player for the legendary 'Bear' Bryant at the University of Alabama, and then he turned down an opportunity to play in the NFL because he felt called to begin the Ranch instead. That was over forty years ago, and as a result of that decision, thousands of children's lives have been changed for the better. Today, Mr. John has handed off the reins to his children Reagan and Brody and their spouses, and he spends much of his time either meeting with kids at the school or traveling around and speaking to various audiences. I have had the privilege of hearing him speak on numerous occasions, and I have always come away challenged and inspired.

In particular, Mr. John has used one phrase on numerous occasions that has stuck with me and that is applicable here: "A man with experience is never at the mercy of a man with an argument." After saying that, he would go on to explain many of the ups and downs he has gone through in over forty years of mentoring and helping children who come from very difficult circumstances. When someone comes to him with what seems like a great idea, or a brand-new plan that will solve lots of problems, he can listen patiently and evaluate their information in light of almost half a century of experience of working with children. Having lived through many years of running this ministry, he has the experience necessary to make informed decisions about every area of the Ranch, and he has spent the past several years passing on much of that information to his children. The Croyle family is an excellent example of how experience is extremely important in helping us as leaders determine what our values are and how we're going to implement them.

Part IV: Find The Balance

Experience matters, but it is often limited in scope. Education is important, but it alone is not enough. So as a leader what we need to be doing is finding the balance between education and experience. We need to be continually looking for learning opportunities, to be learning from other people. We also need to be experiencing what it is our audience or followers are going through. If I seem to be losing touch with my audience or followers, it may be because I am not spending enough time doing what they do, and thus I lose perspective on the practical side of things. When that happens, my leadership loses its effectiveness.

A final aspect of how humility relates to a willingness to learn is that we must take the time to truly listen whenever our audience or followers bring us a problem or issue, even if we think it is minor. Rather than simply assuming we already have the answer, we must take time to hear the problem out; when we do that, we may realize that the nature of the problem is different than we assumed.

Many great military leaders, including George Washington, have said things such as, "Never ask your troops to do anything that you wouldn't do." There is a lot of wisdom in that statement, and we as leaders need to remember that. We need to balance our practical knowledge (experience) with our theoretical knowledge (education), and as always we need to remember that, when in doubt we should err on the side of service and humility, just as Christ said He came not to be served but to serve.

"Growing in our knowledge of God changes our view of everything else." - Dr. Kelly Kapic

Questions to Consider

1. Which is more important: education or experience? Why do you think that?

2. Do you think that a leader should lead based on what they know or what they have done? Why?

3. In what ways does your knowledge of the Gospel shape your leadership?

Action Step:

Spend some time writing down three ways in which your education and experience shape your leadership.

Chapter 8

Your Biggest Mistakes Are Still to Come: Hard Truths of Leading and Life

It would be wonderful to be able to say that after reading this book you'll never make a mistake or have any trouble in your leadership roles. It would also really be a boost to my pride and ego! And it would be entirely false. The truth is that we will all mess up again tomorrow, and we've probably already messed up today. That is where, especially as leaders, we must embrace the wonderful power of forgiveness found in the Gospel while also not falling prey to what Bonhoeffer referred to as "cheap grace." We are forgiven, certainly, but let us not presume upon Christ's sacrifice and use it as an excuse to sin. We'll sin plenty without having to try!

Part I: "Cheer Up: Things Are Worse Than You Think!"

Just a couple of years ago, I heard my old high school soccer coach, Erik McDaniel, give a speech at our alma mater, Covenant College. During his talk, he said a line that really stuck with me and which I have unashamedly borrowed in many of my speeches since then. He said, "Cheer up: things are worse than you think!" That line struck me because it didn't make any sense in my head until he explained it. However, when he did, it made complete sense and revealed much hidden wisdom. On its surface, the comment doesn't sound encouraging, but here's what he meant by that: there is no such thing as a perfect or flawless leader, or a perfect life. So, especially for young leaders, it is important to recognize that your biggest mistakes are still ahead of you. The biggest pains you will suffer, the harshest lessons you will learn, those are all still to come. And perhaps the biggest lesson that we as leaders have to come to grips with is this: you will fail. You will let people down. You will not accomplish all that you set out to do. But here is the good news and the hidden wisdom in Erik's statement: how you respond to your failures is just as important as the failures themselves. So, cheer up, because it's worse than you think, but through God's grace and in His timing, it will also get better eventually.

In my classroom, we often focus on many of the great leaders of various time periods, men and women from all over the world. One thing they all have in common is that they accomplished great things despite being greatly flawed. There is no such thing as a perfect leader, whether you're talking about Elizabeth I of England (the 'Virgin Queen' from chapter three), or George Washington, Napoleon Bonaparte, Marie Curie, or Mohandas Gandhi, or whoever else you want to discuss. Every leader you study, every great person throughout history is flawed, and if you read their biographies you will find this to be true.

Some biographies are more positive and will focus on their accomplishments and minimize their flaws; others, especially more recent (and often more sensationalized) biographies will choose to focus much more on the negatives, taking great heroes and almost dismissing their accomplishments in favor of "outing" them or focusing on their flaws in order to make an example or 'dispel the myths' of their greatness. Either way, the truth is that there is no such thing as a perfect leader outside of Jesus Christ. He is the only person to ever live a life of perfection, sinless, in complete alignment with what God called Him to do. For us, while we are certainly being transformed to be more and more like Christ, it is also important to remember that we will not be perfect on this side of eternity. Rather, for us the goal is always to be improving, to be growing and to be learning.

In the book *When Breath Becomes Air*, the late Dr. Paul Kalanithi describes his mindset in terms of becoming a neurosurgeon and coming to grips with the fact that perfection is never attainable and yet it remains the goal. He said this: "Our patients' lives and identities may be in our hands, yet death always wins. Even if you are perfect, the world isn't. The secret is to know that the deck is stacked, that you will lose, that your hands or judgment will slip, and yet still struggle to win for your patients. You can't ever reach perfection, but you can believe in an asymptote toward which you are ceaselessly striving." (pg. 115)

Full disclosure: I had to look up what "asymptote" meant after reading that for the first time. The easiest way to describe it is to think of a line or curve that is aimed at and approaching "perfect" without ever reaching it. Here we see an extremely important leadership principle: *in this life, we will never attain perfection, yet as leaders we have a responsibility to strive for it at all times.* Knowing we cannot be perfect is no excuse for failing to attempt perfection anyway. As leaders we cannot afford to fall prey to a fatalism or an acceptance that anything less than perfect is good enough. As C.S. Lewis writes, when talking about attempting to exercise virtue, "The only fatal thing is to sit down content with anything less than perfection."

Part II: You Will Fail.

So if we accept this reality that we will fail, if we accept that it is true, that does not mean that we stop striving for perfection. It means that we focus on trying to fail as little as possible, and it means trying to recognize ahead of time the areas in which we might fail and trying to be proactive about improving those areas. But we must begin by accepting that we will fail. While this is not fun or enjoyable, it is crucial to acknowledge the truth of it if we are to improve.

First, you will fail in little ways everyday, whether that is in a harsh interaction with a child, or a small moment of forgetfulness; whatever it may be, there are times every single day in which we will fail. One of the most difficult aspects for me is when I fail regarding my kids: sometimes I speak harshly with them when I shouldn't, sometimes I forget things that are important to them, and then my task as a father is to model repentance to them. It becomes my duty and joy to sincerely apologize, to ask forgiveness, and then to set about doing what I can to make things right. I will also admit that, when this happens in the classroom or the soccer field, it is much more "duty" than "joy." It's never fun to admit I was wrong in front of a group of my students or players, and yet it is what the Gospel calls me to do.

So when we see those little moments of failure, when we come to grips with the fact that failure is a part of leadership, then our focus should be on, "How do we grow from this? How do we learn from this?" Look at these little failures as opportunities to grow as a leader and as a person, so that we can improve and do better when our next opportunity presents itself.

Second, sometimes our failures will be much bigger: it may be in losing an important game, losing a huge sale, failing to close an important deal or solidify an account, or it may be in harming a relationship. In my life, I've done all of those things at different times. For example, as I mentioned earlier in the book, the high school soccer team I coach has lost the state championship game two years in a row. The first time, two years ago, the girls were undefeated for the entire season, going 24-0 before losing that final. To win that game and go 25-0 would have meant completing one of the greatest high school sports seasons in Alabama soccer history.

Instead, we fell at the final hurdle; it was a tremendous blow, and at first it felt like a failure. Looking back on it, going 24-1 and finishing as state finalists is the opposite of failure: those girls had a tremendously great season! But it didn't feel like it at the time.

For us to get past the pain of that loss, it required remembering what our focus truly is as a program: our ultimate goal is not just to win games but to use soccer to become more like Christ. And as most people know, we often learn more from our failures and losses than we do from our victories. The bigger the stakes, the harder and more lasting the lessons learned. So now, we look at that season and we're excited to remember a number of key victories from it: our players improved as players; we improved as a team; the girls experienced friendships and relationships that will last far beyond high school; and they were successful in the classroom (every senior graduated). In light of eternity, and even in this life, every one of those things are more important than winning or losing a single game, even a state championship.

I also know that a lot of people reading this can identify with what it is like to harm or fail in a relationship. I am divorced and now remarried, and I'm not sure that there are a whole lot of things in life more painful than seeing a marriage fall apart, especially when that happens largely due to my own mistakes. As a leader, you may not experience failure in all of these areas, but you will go through times in which you will harm the things that you hold most dear, you will hurt the people that you value the most, and then the question becomes: how will you respond in those moments?

Are you going to become bitter? Are you going to become frustrated and angry long-term? Or are you going to stick to the principles and values that you believe in, trying to learn from and build from that failure so that you can do better next time? Will you remember the Gospel of grace and ask God to help you live it out better tomorrow than you did today? Remember, as a leader you will fail. How you respond to that failure will in large part shape the type of leader that you become in the long run. Everyone fails. But it's quitting or giving up trying that is the real failure. As World War II hero and U.S. Army General George S. Patton said, "Success is how high you bounce when you hit bottom." You will fail, but you yourself are not a failure until you give up trying to improve.

Part III: You Will Be Underappreciated, Unrecognized, And Criticized For Your Efforts.

Another hard truth about leadership is that most of what you do will be unappreciated or unrecognized. That is, a lot of your work and effort as a leader will simply go unnoticed or be taken for granted. Anyone reading this who is a parent, teacher, coach, or volunteer is likely nodding his/her head right now when thinking of how often you are taken for granted. That is just the reality of being a leader; these are things that you are going to have to accept if you are going to lead.

Think of Christ and how He was taken for granted by the crowds who came to Him for food or for healing, without really wanting to hear what He had to say. Another obvious way to illustrate this point is to think of the many things our parents or other adults did for us when we were children that we did not recognize until we had children of our own. These are things such as making lunches when we were too young, washing our laundry, driving us to and picking us up from various events, attending our extracurricular activities and functions, helping us with our homework when we didn't understand it…. the list could go on forever.

As a child, it never occurred to me that these things were voluntary and that I should show true appreciation for them. I just assumed that those were things that parents were supposed to do. Now that I have two daughters of my own, I recognize that all of those things took time and effort, and I should have done a much better job of telling my mom and dad how much I appreciated all that they did for me. When I realized this a couple of years ago, I did actually call and speak to my mom about it. Unfortunately, and to my lasting shame, I am not sure if I ever truly told my dad how much I appreciated him before he passed away. Remember that as a leader, much of what you do will be taken for granted. Accept that up front, and it becomes easier to not get so frustrated by it down the road.

The next harsh truth to be aware of here is that you will be criticized by people with very little knowledge or experience in your area of expertise and leadership. In a recent chapel service at my high school, the football coach was speaking, and he mentioned how part of coaching is accepting that everyone in the stands thinks they know more than you do. And he's right! Just think of the amount of time casual fans spend criticizing everyone from volunteer youth coaches to professional coaches who are paid millions of dollars per year. Or ask any teacher how many times parents with no teaching experience tell them how they ought to be doing things in their classroom. And this is not even to mention the amount of criticism teachers get from students about how they run their classes!

Recently I heard a friend comment, "Every man thinks he is the expert at two things: coaching football and grilling meat." And if we're honest with ourselves, we all tend to act that way about certain things. We criticize those with much more experience and expertise in certain areas, and we rarely stop to ask ourselves whether our criticism is justified; instead, we just carry on as if it was perfectly normal. So, the truth is that when we are in those positions of leadership, we must expect criticism to come, and we must already know ahead of time how we are going to respond to it, especially when it comes from those who are entirely unqualified to criticize.

Part IV: How You Respond Is Crucial.

One of the key themes of this book is Confident Humility, trusting in God and the talents He has given you while remaining self-aware enough to understand that you always have more to learn. Thus, the proper response in situations in which we are being underappreciated, unrecognized, or outright criticized is to respond with humility, patience, respect, and kindness, especially when those traits are absent from the criticism we are receiving. Admittedly, this is easy to write and very difficult to do; yet it remains the proper response. In the moments when I am being criticized by parents for various reasons, I have found that listening respectfully often brings their emotions down, and this allows me to then enlist the parent as an ally in addressing whatever their concerns may be.

If that is a student who isn't getting his work done, and a parent complains to me about how I need to do a better job of monitoring this, then I will listen and try to get the parent to help me figure out the proper response. The key is, am I listening to the parent's concern, or am I immediately looking to correct or contradict the parent? I will also fully admit that this is one of my largest areas of failure in my leadership: that is, I tend to get defensive when I am criticized, and this is yet another result of my pride. Fortunately, God isn't done with me yet.

Or think of it another way: referees probably have the most thankless task in all of sports, just as managers often have the most thankless task in the workplace because if they do their jobs well they are often unnoticed; if they do their jobs poorly they become the best-known people around. The job of both is to help monitor others to make sure that they are accomplishing things in the proper way, and that means a large part of the job is intervention and correction, neither of which most people enjoy. I know for me, most of the time I am corrected my first thought is not, "Gee, I'm sure glad someone pointed out my mistake." That may come later, but only with humility. Generally, our response to people like referees and managers is much less positive.

As a coach, what I have found out is that yelling at referees doesn't ever actually help; it only makes my program and me look bad, especially since we have 'Christian' in our school's name. Whether fairly or not, when we label ourselves that way, we are held to a higher standard by those around us, and thus when we fail people take more notice. This is crucial to remember in your own leadership roles, especially if you're going to be around sports. I've never had anyone, referee or student, come back to me and say, "Thanks for talking to me like I was an idiot. You're entirely right, and thanks to your sarcasm I now see things your way so we'll just go with that." What I have done is that I have tried to learn to approach referees more respectfully because even if I disagree with their calls, referees are still people. They have regular jobs, they have families, and they have feelings like everyone else: their calls are not a personal reflection on me, nor on themselves, no matter how much I may disagree with the calls. I need to be humble enough to remember that I am not the one refereeing the game; my job is not to do their job.

As leaders, then, when we are responding to criticism, we need to make sure that we are responding in truth and love. And if we cannot do that, then the best option available is to simply not respond to the critics. I recently read a great blog post from a writer who said that he had published a book that had gotten dozens of positive reviews, but when he received one negative review that is the one that stuck with him. And this review continued to bother him, until he realized he should do two things: 1) ignore it, or 2) use it as motivation to try to be a better writer next time.

This is what we need to do as well. We must be humble enough to ask ourselves, "Is there any truth or validity to this criticism?" Even when the criticism comes from an 'unqualified' source, we must have the humility of Christ and be willing to honestly ask if there is truth in what was said. If there is, then regardless of the way in which the criticism was given to us--that is, even if the criticism was given very rudely or disrespectfully--we need to be willing to admit that and try to address, fix, or overcome the problem pointed out to us.

Much of this chapter may seem like a paradox: we are supposed to lead well while knowing we're going to fail; we know we're going to fail, but we strive for perfection anyway. One of the great writers on leadership, Dr. Kent Keith, published something back in 1968 that I feel is very applicable here called "The 10 Paradoxical Commandments of Leadership."

1. People are illogical, unreasonable, and self-centered. Love them anyway.
2. If you do good, people will accuse you of selfish ulterior motives. Do good anyway.
3. If you are successful, you win false friends and true enemies. Succeed anyway.
4. The good you do today will be forgotten tomorrow. Do good anyway.
5. Honesty and frankness make you vulnerable. Be honest and frank anyway.
6. The biggest men with the biggest ideas can be shot down by the smallest men with the smallest minds. Think big anyway.
7. People favor underdogs but follow only top dogs. Fight for a few underdogs anyway.
8. What you spend years building may be destroyed overnight. Build anyway.
9. People really need help but may attack you if you do help them. Help people anyway.
10. Give the world the best you have and you'll get kicked in the teeth. Give the world the best you have anyway.

"Success is stumbling from failure to failure with no loss of enthusiasm." - Winston Churchill

Questions to Consider

1. What has been your biggest leadership failure, and how can you avoid making similar mistakes in the future?

2. When have you experienced a situation that ended up being worse than you thought, and how did you respond?

3. What do you think is the best way to respond to leadership situations in which you fail?

Action Step:

Consider Christ's response to our sin, and write down three ways in which you can better respond to failures in your life than you have in the past.

Chapter 9

"Make Each Day Your Masterpiece" (Coach John Wooden): Reason to Hope

As Christians we have the joy of knowing that life is a blessing and a gift from God. We have the joy of the Gospel and the knowledge that, no matter how much we fail here, no matter how bad things get, that in the final assessment God wins. And because we have that joy, even though we won't experience it fully this side of eternity, yet because of the work of Christ we have reason to hope.

Part I: Lead Where You Are.

Despite some of the negativity or potentially discouraging aspects of what we've seen in this book, there are many reasons to hope for the future. There are many positive stories out there, and I encourage you to be one. Remember that it is not the size of your audience that matters, but rather it is the size of your impact. My wife recently told me about a story she saw in the news about a couple that has been married for over thirty years, and they have eight biological children. What they have also done for the past few years is to adopt terminally ill young foster children, so that those children can spend their last days in a home with a family. So far, they have adopted at least six, and they currently are fostering a toddler who has irreparable brain damage. This is an amazing example of showing the love of Christ to "the least of these."

At first glance, this may not seem like it's making a huge impact in the world, adopting one terminally ill child at a time. But stop and think for a second about the impact that display of love is having on each of the eight biological children; now imagine how far that impact will go through those eight children and also the news story that has now been seen by tens or even hundreds of thousands of people. There is no way to measure the impact that family will have, inspiring and encouraging other families to work with or adopt foster children, terminally ill children, work in an animal shelter, or any other way of creating and pursuing good in the world. It all started with one family making the choice to impact one area of the world, focusing on one very small audience, and the impact will be felt for years. As I said, there are positive stories out there. So let us each be one! Let us impact the future by rethinking leadership in light of the Gospel and by helping other leaders to do the same.

Over Christmas break 2017, I was in the waiting room of a chiropractor's office waiting my turn to see the doctor. As I was waiting, there was another story on a local news channel about a man who until recently had been working in an upscale bar and restaurant, one which sold bottles of water for up to $20. As he told his story, he recounted how one day it occurred to him that while he was selling expensive water that people sometimes left unopened, many people around the world suffer and die due to not having any clean water available to them. Not long after that, he left his job in order to address that issue, and so now he spends his time bringing water to parts of the world that otherwise wouldn't have any. Seeing the suffering of others contrasted with the luxury in which he worked caused him to want to make a change that would serve and impact others far beyond his job in the restaurant. In doing this, he has become a great example of the first principle of Confident Humility: Lead Where You Are.

Where the man found himself was working in a restaurant, and that position prepared him to lead there and then elsewhere, looking at how he could do things differently to make an impact on others. This example should also cause us to evaluate our own situation and locations and ask, "What can I do, where I am, to make an impact?"

If we all improve our little pocket of the world every day, the overall impact will not remain little. It will be tremendous. Most of leadership is seen in the small moments: daily discussions, quiet interactions, small gatherings. Who knows how many people the man mentioned above served in the restaurant, or interacted with there? How many expensive bottles of highly priced water went unopened or unfinished? How many people bought them and didn't think twice about having access to water? And then one day, something clicked, and he made a huge change. If we pay attention, we realize that in the small moments we are being prepared for the big moments and changes that will come our way.

Part II: Lead Through Learning.

On this side of eternity, in our broken and fallen world, there will always be room for improvement. Thus the second principle of Confident Humility is this: Lead Through Learning. As the previous chapter stated, there is no such thing as a perfect leader, and thus there is always room for improvement. The former NBA star Michael Jordan often spoke about his success and how it was a result of the relentless pursuit of perfection. His goal was always to play a perfect game: every pass perfect, every shot perfect, every aspect of the game perfect. He never attained it, but the pursuit of that perfection is what allowed him to be such a success, and it is no surprise the he is considered one of the best basketball players of all-time.

This should also be our goal every day. Or, put another way as did John Wooden: "Make each day your masterpiece." Every day we can learn more, we can grow more, we can serve more. One of the ways to do this is to look to mentors, whether real or virtual. What I mean by virtual mentors is the group of people that we consciously study from afar via biographies and individual research: study their lives, figure out what makes them tick, and then pattern our lives after them in such a way that we become like them, just as Paul instructed various churches to do in the New Testament. There are more learning avenues available today than ever before thanks to the Internet. We have more opportunities to learn than any people in history, so let us take advantage of those opportunities to become better leaders.

This also means that it is never too late to start learning and start changing. One historical example of this is George Wallace, the former governor of Alabama. I've grown up in Alabama, and therefore I have observed firsthand--though, not being a minority, I have not experienced firsthand--the latent cultural effects of slavery and racism, of Jim Crow and segregation in Alabama. George Wallace was governor of Alabama during much of the Civil Rights era, and for years he was a symbol of many of those negative cultural aspects of Alabama. In 1963, during his inaugural address as governor he said the infamous line, "Segregation now, segregation tomorrow, segregation forever." And throughout the rest of the 1960s, he was strongly opposed to any kind of changes in favor of civil rights, any changes in the political, cultural, and social status quo in Alabama.

And yet, later in his life George Wallace came to realize that his views and his treatment of other people were wrong, and he was able to overcome his previous beliefs. He even committed what would today be considered political suicide: without any prompting that I've ever heard of, he publicly came forward and admitted that he had been wrong, and he sought out ways to try to reconcile with the people that he had hurt. Do a quick Google search for "George Wallace change of heart," and you will find articles from the New York Times, the Washington Post, the Tuscaloosa News, the Huffington Post, the Baltimore Sun, and other media outlets all about how George Wallace repented and changed. CNN even called him, "A man with the courage to change."

He was not afraid to admit that he had been wrong, he apologized for doing his best to block the integration of public schools, and he eventually became a symbol of reconciliation in Alabama. At the University of Montevallo, a number of buildings are named for both him and his wife, Lurleen, who succeeded him as governor. In fact, for almost fifty years, she remained the only female governor of the state of Alabama. It's never too late to start, it's never too late to learn, and it's never too late to change. The old adage of, "You can't teach an old dog new tricks" may or may not be accurate when applied to canines; it is only accurate about people when we allow it to be.

Hopefully we don't have to undergo as drastic a change as George Wallace, though if we examine our hearts there may be areas in which we need such a large change. If that's the case, there is no better time to begin making that change than today. Start small, with a single interaction, but however we start, let us continue to lead through learning and let us start today.

Part III: Be The First.

Choose the good and do what needs to be done. The third and final principle of Confident Humility is very simple: Be the First.

In the beloved book series *The Chronicles of Narnia*, there are numerous examples of what it means to be a great leader. One example is of the child Edmund, who in the original book *The Lion, the Witch, and the Wardrobe*, betrays his family to the evil White Witch. In a later book, *The Horse and His Boy*, Edmund is discussing whether or not to execute an unscrupulous foreign prince named Rabadash who was captured after attempting to secretly invade and attack Archenland and Narnia despite peace agreements between the kingdoms. Edmund says an amazingly humble statement in defense of not executing Rabadash when he states, referring to himself and his actions in *The Lion, the Witch, and the Wardrobe*, "Even a traitor may mend. I have known one who did." That type of humility, self-awareness, and willingness to choose to see the potential for good may be beyond most of us. Most people do not like to think that someone who has betrayed us could mend, could become trustworthy again. But that is the whole point of this section: as leaders, we need to be the first to choose to see the good in people, just as God continues to see Christ in us despite our sin, and who sent Christ to die for us even before we repented.

We must focus on seeing not just the good that already exists, but choose to see the good that is only there in potential. There is another great quote from that same book where another character, King Lune of Archenland describes his view of leadership. He says, "For this is what it means to be king: to be the first in every desperate attack and last in every desperate retreat. And when there is hunger in the land, as must be now and then in bad years, to wear finer clothes and laugh louder over a scanty meal than any man in your land."

To be a king or queen, to be a leader, means that you are the first person to take responsibility, to stand up against injustice, to serve people that need serving. It means you are often the last one to leave, whether that is a desperate retreat or simply a meeting when there are things to be cleaned up afterward. It means that when things are not good ("when there is hunger in the land"), that leaders must be the first to choose the good anyway.

As U2 frontman Bono recently said, "Joy is the ultimate act of defiance." In a broken and sinful world, full of pain and suffering and bitterness and anger, joy most certainly is an act of defiance. When there is hunger in the land, leaders choose to be joyful anyway, in defiance of the circumstances. To be a leader is to act as if things are better than they are, knowing that things are rarely as bad as they seem. This is not done in order to deceive people; rather it is done to encourage people by our example. When my father was losing his battle to cancer ten years ago, I remember being amazed at the fact that each time I went to check on him, each time I visited him at home or in the hospital, his first action was to ask me about how my family was doing and to downplay what he was going through. Most people have experienced something similar with a sick loved one: when you check on them you feel sorry for them because of what they are going through, but you leave feeling encouraged because of their attitude and positivity in the midst of suffering.

As leaders we must, like King Lune, choose the good in every situation, and we can start doing that today. How can you serve? Who can you serve? And how can we influence the next generation of leaders to be more humble and more selfless? The answer is very simple: be the first. Don't wait on someone else to point out the good; go and find it and share it with others. Be the first to influence others positively by choosing the good and pointing people to Christ through how you relate to them.

In the movie version of *The Lord of the Rings: The Two Towers*, the character Sam Gamgee has one of the greatest, most encouraging and challenging lines in film history. The characters are on a long and dangerous journey, they have had many chances to turn back, and yet they kept going. At one point, Frodo has reached a point of desperation, and he asks Sam why they keep going, what they are holding onto. And Sam's answer is spectacular when he says, "There is some good in this world, Mr. Frodo, and it's worth fighting for." That was true for them in Middle-Earth, and it is true for us as well. *The Lord of the Rings* is my favorite book of all time, and I also love the movies for many reasons. Every time I watch this scene, I am moved because it is exactly right: despite the sin and brokenness, despite the heartache and pain, there is good in this world, and it is worth fighting for.

Leadership will not be easy. It is not for the faint of heart. It will be hard, it will be a struggle and a fight. People that you lead will resist your efforts, especially when you challenge the status quo. People will criticize your efforts and not accept your explanations for your choices. It will be difficult, but it is worth fighting for the good. In the excellent movie *A League of Their Own*, actor Tom Hanks's character is rebuking a player for quitting when things got hard. He says to her, "It's the hard that makes it great. If it was easy, everyone would do it." This is a line I quote every semester to my students and every season to my athletes. Leadership is hard, and it's the hard that makes it great. Let us take the proper approach when we do it: be confident in God's goodness and the gifts He has given you, be humble in the way you relate to other people, and always, always, always, fight for the good.

"All we have to decide is what to do with the time that is given us."
- J.R.R. Tolkien

Questions to Consider:

1. **Why do we as believers have reason to hope, and how can we share that hope with the world around us?**

2. **Other than Christ, what are some examples of "good" in your world that are worth fighting for, and how will you fight for them?**

3. How can you take steps to remain humble in your relationships and leadership roles?

Action Step:

Write down what you think is Christ's greatest gift to you, and post it somewhere that you will see it on a daily basis.

Made in the USA
Middletown, DE
27 November 2022

15962101R00073